INTELLECTUAL CAPITAL

INTELLECTUAL CAPITAL

Money and Mind at St John's College, Oxford

MATTHEW FORD

PROFILE
EDITIONS

First published in Great Britain in 2023 by
Profile Editions, an imprint of
Profile Books Ltd
29 Cloth Fair
London
EC1A 7JQ
www.profileeditions.com

Copyright © Saint John Baptist College in the University of Oxford, 2023

1 3 5 7 9 10 8 6 4 2

Typeset in Garamond by MacGuru Ltd
Printed and bound in Great Britain by
Clays Ltd, Elcograf S.p.A.

The moral right of the author has been asserted.

All rights reserved. Without limiting the rights under copyright reserved above, no part of this publication may be reproduced, stored or introduced into a retrieval system, or transmitted, in any form or by any means (electronic, mechanical, photocopying, recording or otherwise), without the prior written permission of both the copyright owner and the publisher of this book.

A CIP catalogue record for this book is available from the British Library.

ISBN 978 1 800818 552

Contents

Preface vii

1. This is the Record of John — 1
2. Et in Arcadia Ego — 71
3. The Avalanche — 111
4. A Little Learning — 139
5. Arrangements Around the Fact — 167

Epilogue — 187
Appendix: History from Below — 193

Bibliography — 197
Index — 213

PREFACE

When the idea for a financial history of St John's College was first suggested to me, I remember saying that it would be very interesting to know the answers to the questions posed – where did the College get its money? How badly did it mismanage it? How important was the money in its academic ascent? – but we were certainly going to struggle to find anyone who'd be willing to take on such a boring project. I'm delighted that I overcame that initial prejudice, and I hope you will find this exploration as interesting as I have.

Many people have helped in writing this book. William Whyte and John Kay have been excellent supervisors, giving me all the support I needed but complete freedom to structure the project as I wanted. Michael Riordan has been a fount of information on all aspects of the St John's archive, and has uncomplainingly put up with getting emails at all hours of the day and night. All the members of St John's SCR have been unfailingly kind, generous, and supportive of me: in particular the fabulous SCR staff who have had to put up with me coming to dinner far too often. In addition to giving permission for me to use one of their poems as a chapter title, Minying Huang provided invaluable feedback on the manuscript and quite possibly saved my life in Argentina.

I am particularly thankful – for all sorts of different forms of support, advice, and information – to Ronald Barnes, Simon Baynham, Louise Benson, Susan Black, David Cannadine,

Sarah Charlton, Douglas Crichton, Robin Darwall-Smith, Aled Davies, Elroy Dimson, Yannick Ford, Zoe Hancock, William Hayes, Simon Jenkins, Georgy Kantor, Giles Mandelbrote, Leslie Mitchell, Avner Offer, Natalie Quinn, Harry Reddish, Georgina Robinson, Michael Scholar, Mishka Sinha, Margaret Snowling, Katherine Southwood, Ana Maria Stoienescu, Reinier van Straten, Keith Thomas, and Nicholas Woodhouse. I am also grateful to Paris Arnold (matriculated 1990), John Atkins (m. 1974), Tim Connolly (1978–81), A. D. Harvey (m. 1966), Kishor Kale (m. 1983), Geoffrey Penzer (m. 1962), Harvey Pitcher (m. 1957), and Steve Postle (m. 1969) for sending their memories of their time at St John's and giving a richer sense of what it was like to be a student over the years. And I am grateful to Eton College, the Howard de Walden Estate, and Lambeth Palace for allowing me to use their archives.

Finally, I want to thank St John's for funding the project. I spent three deliriously happy years here as an undergraduate; it has been lovely to add a fourth.

1

THIS IS THE RECORD OF JOHN

How St John's Built and Lost a Fortune

> Everyone knows of course that the real history of a college year cannot be set down. What is really happening to the minds of any number of our community of 400 scholars is obviously more important than jottings about 'emergent' points of interest. Yet the latter can be known and the former cannot. A point against historians.
>
> College Record, 1971

In 1855 the news reached the Fellows of St John's College, Oxford, that the private Act of Parliament they had requested had received Royal Assent. The text was laconic: 'An Act to enable the President and Scholars of *Saint John Baptist* College in the University of *Oxford* to grant Building Leases of their Lands in the Parishes of *Saint Giles, Saint Thomas*, and *Woolvercot, Oxford*; and for other Purposes.'[1] Why, in the middle of the nineteenth century, was an Oxford college seeking to become a property developer? Why did Parliament have to give its permission? And who were the 'President and Scholars' anyway?

---

1 Shadwell (1912) p. 339. The Act dates from 14 August 1855.

The answers would shape the future of Oxford: architecturally, financially, and intellectually.

The Early Years

St John's, a college in the University of Oxford, was founded in 1555 by Sir Thomas White: a cloth merchant in London who eventually became Master of the Merchant Taylors, the Company for people in his profession. White was also a pious Catholic and his College was designed to train Catholic clergy to promulgate England's counter-Reformation under Mary I. This might have seemed an unfortunate decision when Mary died in 1558 and Elizabeth I swung the country back to Protestantism. Worryingly, the College was founded in the same year that Bishops Latimer, Ridley, and Cranmer were burnt to death just two minutes' walk from its only quadrangle. Fortunately Elizabeth I was a less bloodthirsty ruler, and St John's transitioned to training Protestant clergy (losing its second President, who could not reconcile himself to the change, along the way).[2]

The College was initially quite poor and relied on handouts from its Founder – which became increasingly sparse as his fortunes declined towards the end of his life.[3] Originally intended to be a community of fifty poor scholars, it hovered around twenty-five until 1583, when the College's financial footing had improved somewhat.[4]

What was it like to live and study here? A typical student in the sixteenth century might be the aspirational but not especially

---

[2] Stevenson and Salter (1939) pp. 130, 323.
[3] Ibid. p. 141. Reports of the Founder's poverty have sometimes been exaggerated – he died with plenty of property, just not as much as at his peak.
[4] Costin (1958) pp. 1–2; Stevenson and Salter (1939) p. 208.

well-off son of a merchant. They would probably come up to the College while they were still young – perhaps sixteen years old – having already been educated at a school connected with the College such as Merchant Taylors' in London.[5] After arriving in Oxford they would go through the North Gate and leave the city walls behind them, and after passing the centuries-old foundation of Balliol and walking halfway along a building they would turn in at a great door under a tower, perhaps glancing up at a statue of St John the Baptist in a niche above the entrance. Opening in front of them was a fairly large gravelled quadrangle. Behind and to their right were sandstone buildings with rooms and studies for tutors and students; directly ahead were the new President's Lodgings; and to their left lay the chapel and the Hall. (The battlements – ornamental rather than defensive, a status symbol for a prosperous college – were merely glimmers of possibility at this point.[6] They were erected following a gift of £150 from Thomas and Benjamin Henshaw in 1618.[7]) The only sound disturbing the studious atmosphere would be the gentle cooing of pigeons from the pigeon house behind the Lodgings (at least until 1599: the Fellows declared it was 'unprofitable and otherwise very ruinouse' and that a new one should be built 'in some more commodiouse place', but this never seems to have happened).[8]

The buildings would have looked too old for such a new college – in fact they had been taken and repurposed from St Bernard's College. This Cistercian foundation dated from 1437

---

[5] You might be even younger – Stevenson and Salter (1939) p. 169 mentions undergraduates of eleven and older.
[6] Coulson (1982).
[7] Costin (1958) p. 31.
[8] Stevenson and Salter (1939) pp. 300–301.

and was intended to be a home for Cistercian monks pursuing academic study, but it was not very successful in this aim. By the time of the Dissolution of the Monasteries the foundation had not even completed the quadrangle, and it made the Cistercians a laughing stock among their fellow monks (people were noting that the mendicants were building all over the place, and the Cistercians felt the slight).[9] They had, however, built wonderful vaulted wine cellars and a kitchen so enormous that, when St John's took over the site, it was repurposed as the Hall.[10] Even the statue of the College's patron saint above the entrance was just a statue of St Bernard transformed by the addition of a plaster beard.[11]

Students would go to college lectures – more like classes, where they might construe passages in Latin or Greek, or tackle a logic problem – and some University ones. Chapel was generally twice daily. They ate in Hall, sitting at a table with their peers – either the other scholars or the commoners (who paid fees to attend the College).[12] Because the aim was to educate future clergy it was necessarily a transient place: some Fellows might remain, playing a dual academic and religious role (or being given an exemption from taking holy orders by studying medicine); but many hoped to serve as priests elsewhere by

---

9 Colvin (1959) pp. 40–41.
10 Ibid.
11 It is unclear when the plaster was first added, but it is plausible that it was early on. The *College Record* for 1915 states that 'some strange plaster accretions of the eighteenth century have been removed' from the statue's head, but those may well have been added when the original plaster fell off. Stevenson examined the statue after it was taken down and found that 'The back of the head seems to have a tonsure ... the garment in front ... is certainly not camel hair, and looks like a monkish garment', confirming that it was originally of St Bernard rather than St John (Stevenson and Salter, 1939, p. 92).
12 Stevenson and Salter (1939) p. 246.

getting a living – which, if it was sufficiently prosperous, disqualified them from their Fellowship.[13] (They might leave for other reasons as well: Edmund Campion, one of the College's most brilliant scholars, charmed Elizabeth I on her royal visit and received patronage from the influential Earl of Leicester. But over time he began to have doubts, and in 1569 he left the University – and Britain. He returned as a Catholic in 1576 and was eventually caught, sentenced, and brutally executed.)

Students might take a degree or they might not, although doing so came with financial incentives. There was much criticism of the academic standards of the University: the cosmologist Giordano Bruno, who had briefly been at the University of Geneva, described it as 'a constellation of ignorant, obstinate pedants: a herd of donkeys and swine', and in 1589 Archbishop Whitgift complained that lectures were often unattended and discipline was despised.[14] But standards may have been higher at St John's as a relatively new foundation; in theory scholars younger than eighteen could be flogged if they did not behave and there were occasions when such a punishment was carried out.[15]

It was at this College that a young student named William Laud arrived in 1589. Laud was the son of a modestly successful clothier from Reading, and was awarded one of the scholarships the Founder had established.[16] We do not know very much about his student life, except that he already held the anti-Puritan views that would shape his life's work and eventually lead

---

[13] Stevenson and Salter (1939) p. 148 notes that a Fellowship at St John's could be kept as long as the living was not worth more than £10, or £15 if the holder was a Doctor of Divinity.

[14] Trevor-Roper (1962) pp. 33–4.

[15] Stevenson and Salter (1939) p. 148.

[16] Trevor-Roper (1962) p. 32.

to his clash with Parliament and his downfall. Those views also led to opposition at Oxford – his detractors claimed he was publicly censured by the Professor of Divinity for being a 'sower of discord among brethren' – but this was insufficient to hold him back, and he became a Fellow and then President.[17] And he turned the tables on his Puritan opponents, transforming St John's into a centre of anti-Puritan doctrine in Oxford. The College's anthem 'This is the Record of John' was composed by Orlando Gibbons at his request – given the Puritans' opposition to organs in churches, he must have found this particularly satisfying.

Laud was, by all accounts, a successful President. Yet nothing became the College like his leaving it – because, as he moved through a series of ecclesiastical appointments before reaching the summit of the English Church as Archbishop of Canterbury, he became the ideal patron. Canterbury Quadrangle, built at his direction and expense, displayed the three qualities most important in patronage: finance, political pull, and learning. The handsome new quadrangle – incorporating pioneering Baroque features, as well as a mixture of classical and Gothic influences – almost doubled the size of the College and provided it with a new mathematical library, which Laud ensured was stocked with a broad range of texts (many in Arabic – Laud was enthusiastic about foreign languages and founded a perpetual chair in Arabic at Oxford) and scientific instruments such as astrolabes.[18] It included magnificent rooms for students (centuries later they were still described as the best in the university), the rents

---

17 Trevor-Roper (1962) p. 39. The accusation comes from William Prynne, who was responsible for Laud's trial in 1640, but since he fabricated so much other evidence about Laud this too may be exaggerated.

18 Colvin (1988) pp. 21, 75.

from which were intended to permanently fund the librarian and augment the College's income.[19] The structure cost £5,554 to build, and another £2,666 was spent on a grand feast given by Laud for Charles I to celebrate its opening in 1636.[20] It was perhaps the greatest feast of his reign: there were cakes shaped to look like members of the University and ecclesiastical hierarchy, vast quantities of meat, and – an exceptional rarity in that period – two plays the royal visitors actually enjoyed watching.[21] Laud also found time to become Chancellor of the University and supervise the rewriting of its statutes, which would guide the institution for the next two centuries and introduced examinations for degrees (an unpopular move with the students, many of whom left for Cambridge to avoid them).[22]

Unfortunately the Archbishop's star had reached its zenith in 1636. Laud had supported his king and his church, most controversially by creating the unpopular Scottish Book of Common Prayer and attempting to impose it upon the Scots. Their reaction was so violent that it was never used. But his changes were not limited to Scotland: 'Laudianism' saw a more high-church style spread across England, and opponents of the changes faced fierce punishments, such as branding and having their ears cropped. When Parliament began to make moves against Charles I, Laud was a natural target. In 1641 he was imprisoned in the Tower of London on charges of treason. He was brought to trial in 1644 but his enemies could not prove their case, despite fabricating evidence against him. Determined that justice be done, whatever the law might say, the House of Commons

---

19 Costin (1958) p. 44; Nichols (1922) p. 109.
20 SJC MUN LXXXI.2.
21 Costin (1958) pp. 41, 46; Trevor-Roper (1962) p. 293.
22 Trevor-Roper (1962) p. 279.

passed an ordinance declaring him guilty and sentencing him to execution. The Lords were persuaded of the righteousness of this manoeuvre by the threat of a mob being set on them if they did not acquiesce.[23] Like his College's patron saint, Laud was beheaded in 1645. He left the College more books and money, wishing that 'God's everlasting blessing be upon that place and that society for ever' – wishes Parliament ignored, giving his library to the chaplain of the army.[24]

The College's connection to Laud, however, lived on. After the monarchy's restoration his body was reburied in the chapel. This seems to have given him a taste for posthumous perambulation. Reports still circulate of him haunting his library and bowling his head down it, and on one occasion an otherwise sober student was seen by his friends 'in a state of terror': 'his face was pale green ... he seemed to be saying, "Oh, the feet, the feet ... in the ceiling" ... When he had calmed down a bit, he told us that he had been to bed and was awakened by a brilliant light in his room, followed by a cold blast of air ... the light was seen to be coming from two vivid legs and feet that marched beneath his ceiling.'[25] There were lights in the library despite everyone's whereabouts being accounted for. When other colleges have had similar issues the affected areas have been blessed, but does any cleric have the authority or power to banish an archbishop?[26]

More poignantly, Laud's pet tortoise happily roamed the

---

23 Trevor-Roper (1962) pp. 422–7.
24 Hutton (1898) p. 154.
25 *College Record* (1974) p. 49.
26 Associated Press (17 Feb 1987). The consensus seems to be that, even setting aside metaphysical and spiritual objections to the existence of ghosts, a martyr of the Church would certainly not be left wandering the Earth – so if there actually *is* a spectre haunting the College's most European quad, it is not the spectre of conservative Laud.

gardens of Lambeth Palace for more than a century after its owner's demise. The animal may have been acquired while he was at St John's, and would doubtless have been a great comfort to the difficult, divisive but dedicated man who, beset with doubts about his own piety, struggled against opponents who were certain that they were in the right.[27]

Spectres of Laud

Laud's death put St John's out of joint; it was also a sign of shifting political sands. The Civil War was in full swing and moving further and further in Parliament's favour. Having lost control of London, Charles I made Oxford his capital, but it was an insecure base. The College's northerly position without the city walls meant it was on the front lines, and may have served as the base for the German princes Rupert and Maurice (nephews of Charles I who took his side in the war). Fortunately the most physical harm that came to it was a single cannon ball which was shot at the tower, and is now preserved in the library. The king escaped that siege, but Oxford would see two more. Nor could the University's loyalty save Charles. The Royalists were defeated and in 1649 he was executed. Attending the monarch in his last moments was Laud's successor as President (and later as Archbishop), William Juxon.

Unsurprisingly Parliament would not let a Royalist college persist, and 'visitors' from London were empowered to replace the President and Fellows with their own men. But the war had financial implications too. Before it the College had been running a substantial surplus; but requests for money from the king meant that it ran up debts and gave away its silver plate,

---

27 I discuss the question of the tortoise's link to St John's further in the Appendix.

while after the war income from students and Fellows fell sharply.[28] Salvation came after the restoration: the Parliamentary president Thankful Owen was himself expelled and the College's friends were able to come to its rescue. Juxon gave £7,000 and even Laud helped, albeit from beyond the grave – £500 promised in his will had been kept safe by his half-brother's son and was given to the College in 1662.[29]

A king was back on the throne. St John's had escaped financial trouble. Its quadrangles no longer echoed with the sounds of armed men (although upon hearing of Monmouth's rebellion against James II in 1685 the loyal College did raise a force in readiness, buying three horses and a variety of weapons 'for ye Coll. Troopers'. They also repaired 'fourscore musketts ... and other Arms of ye Kinge': if, as was typical, the eighty musketeers were complemented by forty pike this would have been a substantial contingent.[30] In the event Monmouth's rebellion was quickly snuffed out and they never saw action; in the very same term there is an item in the accounts 'for ye Prayer book & proclamation for ye Victory over ye Rebels'. The College's ascent – academically, financially, and politically – seemed assured.

But it didn't happen.

The problem was not entirely specific to St John's. The medieval University of Oxford had been an important institution of

---

28 Costin (1958) pp. 97–104.
29 Ibid. p. 125.
30 SJC ACC I.A.49. Pikes performed an important anti-cavalry role for a company of muskets, and in the Civil War both sides aimed to have a ratio of two muskets to each pike – although the pressures of the campaign could alter this either way (Reid, 1998, p. 5). There seems to have been little change by 1685: Childs notes that British companies in the Netherlands in the 1690s were also formed with a 2:1 ratio of muskets to pikes (Childs, 1996, p. 65). I am grateful to Dr Harry Reddish for alerting me to this.

education and scholarly research, but its star was dimming. The coming century would see the well-known criticisms: Gibbon claimed his time at Oxford was 'the most idle and unprofitable of my whole life'; Adam Smith wrote that 'the greater part of the public professors have, for these many years, given up altogether even the pretence of teaching'.[31] And even the most conservative commentators admitted that these criticisms were quite correct.[32] But the rot had set in even earlier.

Contemporaries commented disapprovingly on the state of the University. Anthony Wood, an antiquary, lamented that in the 1666 election for the position of beadle (an officer in the University who supported other officials), the Vice-Chancellor

> desired them by all means that they would not elect a poet ... But notwithstanding this exhortation, which was just, the black-pot-men, or such who are called *boon blades*, who, (with shame be it spoken) carry all before them in elections, did instead of electing a master of arts ... chuse a yeoman-beadle ... who had formerly kept a public inn, and was good for nothing but for eating, drinking, smoking, and punning.[33]

The position had fallen open because the previous incumbent – Edmund Gayton, a Fellow of St John's – had died. This explains the Vice-Chancellor's disapproval of poets: Wood writes that Gayton followed 'the vices of poets, of which number he pretended to be one, and one eminent he might have been, had he not been troubled with the faculty of too much lifting.

---

31 Gibbon (1891) p. 66; Smith (1776) p. 343.
32 Oman (1941) p. 260.
33 Wood (1817) col. 758.

He hath written some good, others most vain and trashy, things', which as a scrupulous chronicler he proceeds to list 'tho' rather fit to be buried in oblivion'.[34]

The new beadle was not the only member of the University overly familiar with alcohol. Eleven years later Humphrey Prideaux, a Student (roughly equivalent to a Fellow) at Christ Church, recorded the visit of the Dutch Admiral van Tromp, who received an honorary doctorate 'but the seaman thinkeing that title out of his element would have nothing to doe with it'.[35] But guided by John Speed, a Fellow of St John's, he soon found something more to his taste:

> Speed stayd in town on purpose to drinke with him, which is the only thing he is good for; and for fear he should loose soe commendable a quality he dayly exerciseth it ... he [van Tromp] confess[ed] that he was more drunke here then [sic.] anywhere else since he came into England, which I thinke very little to the honour of our University. Dr Speed was the chiefe man that encountred him, who mustering up about five or six more as able men as himselfe at wine and brandy got the Dutchman to the Crown Tavern, and there soe plyed him with both that at 12 at night they were fain to carry him to his lodgeings.[36]

Most shamefully, the College was abandoning its original purpose of educating relatively humble students such as Laud. In 1677 they refused to elect Thomas Poke, a boy from Reading,

---

34 Wood (1817) col. 756. The meaning of 'much lifting' is unclear but is probably a reference to drinking.
35 Prideaux (1875) p. 32.
36 Ibid. pp. 32, 35.

as a scholar because he had worked as a mechanic, and suggested that his father was not much better. When the College's Visitor (the ultimate authority in College disputes) heard, he was livid:

> Of some handy craft or other the Grand Seigneur himself is obliged to be, and most of the Apostles were soe ... You think fit to refuse them because they are poor, as if poor meane mens sonnes might not come to be as learned and as pious, and as prudent ... as any greater mens sons.[37]

There were many examples of such men attaining high office in the Church, the Visitor noted, and commanded that Poke be given a place. But the College managed to resist the instruction and Poke had to make do with joining Christ Church.[38]

A few decades later Nicholas Amhurst, a student at St John's, wrote a satire of Oxford morals. His hoary theme was the wiles of women who fraternise with students. The seduction might begin at church – 'Not more debas'd the sabbath was of old,/ When *flocks* and *herds* were in the temple sold' – and continue at a ball:

> At ev'ry round, the am'rous fool to please,
> She feels unblushing the lascivious squeeze;
> Caught by inveigling arts and wily charms,
> He throws himself distracted in her arms;
> The ready priest his curse with marriage crowns,
> He weds, and in a fortnight hangs or drowns.[39]

---

37 Quoted in Costin (1958) p. 152.
38 Ibid. p. 154.
39 Amhurst (1724) pp. 10–12.

The parallels to the class-based exclusion in *Jude the Obscure* are striking, even down to the lack of familial support for an unconventional social choice:

> In wedlock-sheets he stains his gen'rous birth,
> And basely mixes with *plebeian* earth;
> Too late, disheir'd, he vents unfruitful sighs,
> For ever banish'd from his father's eyes.[40]

In his preface Amhurst is explicit about the kind of undesirables a chaste student should avoid: 'the lowest dregs of mankind; the daughters of our *Coblers, Tinkers, Taylors*'.[41] These would-be social climbers 'are not to look above themselves, but to be contented with their own humble condition'.[42] Poorer male students debarred by these attitudes were not missing much. He laments how learning is considered pedantry:

> our *Colleges*, instead of grave philosophers, and *Literati*, swarm with *Smarts* and foplings, that is consummate coxcombs. A College-SMART ... rises at ten, tattles over his tea-table till twelve, dines, dresses, waits upon his mistress, drinks tea again, flutters about in publick, till it is dark, then to the tavern, knocks into college at two in the morning, sleeps till ten again, and disposes of the following day, just as he did of the last ... he huddles over the publick exercises, disputes and passes examination in the sciences after the modern fashion, without understanding a word of what, like a parrot, he is taught memorially to utter ... and

---

40 Amhurst (1724) p. 17.
41 Ibid. p. vi.
42 Ibid. p. vii.

thus passes for a most profound scholar, meerly by being an arrant blockhead.⁴³

Partially as a consequence of these and other writings, Amhurst was expelled from the College and became a prominent critic of William Delaune, the President who presided over his removal.⁴⁴

Amhurst's expulsion, however, was no sign of positive change. The College's reputation probably reached its nadir in 1715 when Delaune sought to be elected to the Lady Margaret Chair in Divinity, for the distinctly unspiritual reason that he needed the income to pay off his notorious gambling debts.⁴⁵ (A previous stint as Vice-Chancellor had already helped by enabling him to 'borrow' £3,000 from the University.⁴⁶) He was successful, having followed the time-honoured Oxonian tradition of packing the election: most of his votes were from 'Bachelors of Divinity, near half of them jail-birds like himself, who had left the University for debt and had not appeared here before in ten years or more. He had rummaged the nation for them.'⁴⁷ Even his

---

43   Amhurst (1724), p. v.
44   Amhurst, quite plausibly, describes the College as a nest of Jacobitism which he would not go along with: 'I had not been there an hour, before King *J–s* the *Third*, the Duke of *Ormond*, my Lord *Bolingbroke, Mar*, and several other such-like healths, together with *confusion to the usurper*, (mentioning his name) and a *speedy restoration* to the *rightful heir*, were proposed in a large company ... I declined them, and therefore begg'd leave in his room to drink King GEORGE. But I was told roundly, that *it was an affront to the company; and that I* ought *to drink what was propos'd to me*' (Amhurst, 1726b, pp. 86–7).
45   Amhurst reports one student 'shaking a box and dice in the theatre, and calling out to him [President Delaune] by name, as he came in, in this manner, *Jacta est alea, doctor, Seven's the main*, in allusion to a scandalous report handed about by the doctors's [sic] enemies, that he was guilty of that infamous practice, and had lost great sums of *other people's* money at dice' (Amhurst, 1726a, p. 3).
46   Costin (1958) pp. 166–8.
47   Stratton in Historical Manuscripts Commission (1901) p. 212.

supporters recognised what they tactfully referred to as his 'misfortunes' but overlooked these as he 'hath a very fine tuneable Voice; whereas Baron [his opponent] is very dull'.[48] Delaune also kept up the tradition of drinking: when he died it was reported that his dropsy 'has not been brought on him by drinking water'.[49]

Amhurst, of course, had an axe to grind. But his criticism of academic standards in the University was mirrored by one of the College's Senior Fellows. Reflecting on his time at the University from 1771 to 1778, Vicesimus Knox noted that Oxford produced little in the way of research and Laud's examinations had degenerated into a farce.[50] Candidates chose their own examiners, and as long as the usual practice of picking friends and 'supply[ing] them well with port' was adhered to, the outcome was a foregone conclusion.[51] Still the form of the ritual had to be observed: and so a series of questions were asked (from a 'Scheme', a little book circulated among the students) and answers given (memorised from the same Scheme). This Scheme was a most valuable aid because, Knox notes, 'The poor young man to be examined in the sciences often knows no more of them than his bedmaker, and the masters who examine are sometimes equally unacquainted with such mysteries.'[52] After a few passages of translation (on the level of 'What is the Hebrew for a skull?'), the examiners, growing tired of the exercise, began to ask questions at random; and when even this was judged to be excessively intellectual they lapsed into conversation on 'the last drinking-bout, or on horses, or read the newspaper, or a novel,

---

48 Hearne (1901) p. 25.
49 Costin (1958) p. 166.
50 Knox (1793) p. 317.
51 Ibid. p. 320.
52 Ibid. p. 319.

or divert themselves as well as they can in any manner, till the clock strikes eleven' and the examination was complete.[53] Higher degrees, he suggested, were much the same. Knox became headmaster of Tonbridge School, evidently having decided that he had more chance of improving young minds there.

The world moved into the nineteenth century, but St John's did not move with it. Thomas Frognall Dibdin, a noted (but not especially scholarly) bibliographer, took his bachelor's degree in 1801. His later work 'swarmed with errors of every description' and even his travel writing was 'flippant, tedious, and inaccurate'.[54] No wonder, given his education:

> lectures had only the air of schoolboy proceedings: nothing lofty, stirring, or instructive was propounded to us. There were no college prizes; and lecture and chapel were all that we seemed to be called upon to attend to ... College exercises were trite, dull, and uninstructive. The University partook of this distressing somnolency. There seemed to be no spur to emulation and to excellence.[55]

Dibdin is a significant figure in the history of St John's, however, because of his (minor) role in setting up an intercollegiate essay society. The aim was for members to give a speech on a topic, such as 'whether the merits or demerits of such a character (Cæsar or Queen Elizabeth, for instance) were the greater?'[56] The Vice-Chancellor himself could not

---

53 Tuckwell (1909) p. 2; Knox (1793) p. 320. Lord Eldon was asked 'What is the Hebrew for a skull?' and gave 'Golgotha' as the answer.
54 Costin (1958) p. 227.
55 Dibdin (1836) pp. 81, 92.
56 Ibid. p. 100.

find anything obviously wrong with the club, and so had to be content with banning it on the grounds that no one knew where such innovations might lead.[57] Other students were more direct, and named the society's members 'the LUNATICS' – a name they took up, noting that 'those who felt no inclination to write essays, or to impose upon themselves the toil of reading and research' would certainly see a diversion 'from dull and hard drinking, frivolous gossip, and Bœotian uproar' as madness.[58] Despite this the club thrived (meeting in college rooms to avoid the Vice-Chancellor's ban) and 'the university itself was eventually benefited by the spirit engendered by such a society. I seem to trace the correction, and reconcoction, of those statutes ... to the spirit awakened by the CONCLAVE OF LUNATICS.'[59] Dibdin was more prescient than he realised: the spirit changed more than just the statutes, though he would not live to see it.

At the turn of the century St John's was more financially stable than it had been, although it had not received many significant donations since the time of Laud and Juxon. Its most exciting venture was a brewery north of the College, where the Beehive is today.[60] (It initially turned a profit but the College ended up subsidising it.[61]) Following its Founder's instructions, much of the land it owned was close to the city of Oxford: mainly farms and meadows, including some directly north of the College (acquired in 1573 when the College bought St Giles and Walton Manor, and in 1636 when it bought a farm in Wolvercote).[62]

---

57 Dibdin (1836) pp. 96–7.
58 Ibid. pp. 103–4.
59 Ibid. p. 105.
60 Stevenson and Salter (1939) pp. 506–7.
61 Costin (1958) p. 146.
62 Ibid. p. 32. For the Wolvercote property deeds and associated documents see SJC MUN XXIX.2–16.

Thus financial stability coexisted with academic stasis. Insofar as things had changed since Laud's time, it was mainly for the worse. Of course a list of anecdotes across the centuries can only tell us so much – but we see few examples of impressive men from the College making their mark on the world in this period, and certainly no one like Juxon or Laud. Even the Hall shows this: the portraits hanging there from this period are, in some cases, of men we know almost nothing about. In no cases are they of men of high academic attainment. Johann Dillenius, appointed as the inaugural Sherardian Professor of Botany at Oxford in 1734 and attached to the College (St John's gave him his Doctor of Medicine degree) was an exception to this record of mediocrity – but apparently he did not merit a portrait. Even Dibdin had to look beyond the College for people interested in really thinking. St John's was conservative by temperament, and seems to have been happy to slumber in the general Oxonian torpor. Change, however, was coming to the University.

A University Reformed

It began at Oriel, a college founded back in 1326. Thanks to the efforts of its Provost, John Eveleigh, an 'Honours' examination for BA candidates was introduced in 1800 – against significant resistance from the University, only overcome by Eveleigh's offer to fund prizes from his own purse. This was the origin of the Class Lists still used today. Despite pioneering this development, Oriel did not put too much faith in the exams and chose new Fellows by picking those who provided the most evidence of 'intellectual capacity' in an internal examination – which often gave different rankings to the Class List. The result was that Oriel was head and shoulders above the other colleges, which were filled with 'port and prejudice ... clubbable whist-playing somnolence'.[63] As we have seen, St John's had been an exemplar of this behaviour, and had no plans to change. While Oriel was girding its intellectual loins, 'Hugh Platt recorded a conversation at St. John's just after the future Dean Stanley had come back from the Holy Land, which he was describing at some length. "Jerusalem be damned", an elderly fellow was heard to observe, "give us wine, women and horses."'[64] But it was certainly not alone: Mark Pattison, later to become Rector of Lincoln College and a key member of the group driving reform in the University, recalled that when colleges had a fellowship vacant

> Each fellow had a vote, and gave it irresponsibly ... The public opinion of the University approved this principle of selection, and had come to regard a college as a club, into which you should get only clubbable men. Then they dispensed each other from the obligation to study for seven years ... the original object of the foundation, the promotion of learning, was wholly abrogated.[65]

Gradually, however, the reforms spread. Balliol also introduced examinations for its Fellowship, and began to acquire a reputation for teaching; it followed this up by introducing entrance examinations for scholarships.[66] University College did not go

---

63 Tuckwell (1907) p. 17.
64 Green (1957) p. 129.
65 Pattison (1885) pp. 74–5. This did not in fact describe the situation at St John's, where the Fellows were either descendants of the Founder or elected by external institutions – but the atmosphere was similar.
66 Jones (2005) pp. 180, 186.

quite so far, but did remove many of the geographical restrictions on Fellowships, getting a better selection of candidates as a result.[67]

We should not imagine that the poor standard of teaching necessarily left undergraduates sympathetic to reform more generally. William Edward Heygate was an exhibitioner (a type of less exalted scholarship) at St John's, having been a pupil at Merchant Taylors', and took a third class in his bachelor's degree in 1839. This effectively meant he had no hope of becoming a Fellow anywhere in Oxford, and although he stayed on to do his MA he became a priest, writing novels to supplement his meagre clerical income and support his wife and eleven children. *Godfrey Davenant: A Tale of School Life* was a surprise hit, and he followed it up with *Godfrey Davenant at College*, clearly based on St John's. The book is not of any great literary merit: it resembles nothing so much as a sine wave, with the protagonist rising, and falling, and rising again, as he hews close to, or strays far from, sound doctrine and good teaching. The characters are the clichés one would expect, carrying not an inner life but a heavy-handed message. For example, one gets a Third rather than a First because he has neglected his studies of Divinity. (He comes to a bad end: 'He was in the third class ... All prospects now of pupils or fellowship were at an end ... he ... joined an inferior radical newspaper, in the columns of which, and at low clubs and tavern meetings, he shone in a lesser sphere, until debt and recklessness drove him from this post also, and he disappeared from the face of society.'[68]) The most exciting event is probably when, as a prank, Godfrey throws over-ripe pears into the wrong man's rooms. Doubtless the novel's prospects

---

67 Brockliss (2016) p. 328.
68 Heygate (1849) pp. 230–31.

were improved by the admiring review of its predecessor in the *English Churchman*, which was confident that it 'cannot fail to have a beneficial influence upon all except the positively vicious, debased, and callous'.[69] Heygate eventually ended up in a reasonable parish in the Isle of Wight, after John Keble (whom we will hear more about shortly) put in a good word for him with Gladstone.[70]

A conservative novel, then: but it is in the preface that we see the full extent of Heygate's opposition to reform. 'The Author desires the ecclesiastical idea to be more fully developed; they seek to destroy it.'[71] As for the proposed reforms:

> If it now seems necessary to demand some knowledge of physical sciences, let us ask ourselves why we have come to this conclusion. Is it our belief, or our deference to the times which influences us? If our belief, do we not also believe that a thorough knowledge of the history of our Church and country is as needful? And, after all, have we not always said, that what we desire to produce at Oxford is not a man knowing all he ought to know, or even a little of all he ought to know, but ποῖος τις, a man of character and capabilities?[72]

The argument is startling to modern readers but was not unusual at the time. Oxford's *raison d'être* was still, for many, explicitly religious. It was here that the debate would be most fierce.

The Tractarians, named for the ninety *Tracts for the Times*

---

69 Quoted in Heygate (1849).
70 Skinner (2004).
71 Heygate (1849) p. vii.
72 Ibid. pp. xii–xiv.

they published, were a group of Anglican dons originating in the Oriel Fellowship concerned with University reform, but in a different direction: they wanted spiritual reformation. The differences between them and the Noetics – another group at Oriel who felt more at home with theological speculation – can be summarised in Tractarian John Keble's comment on leading noetic Richard Whately's common-room talk: his intellectual argumentativeness meant the place 'stank with logic'.[73] Whately in turn had little time for the Tractarians and 'deplored their diversion of the University from its legitimate studies into the mazes of theological controversy'.[74] The movement commenced in 1833 and lost steam in 1845 when John Henry Newman, another leading Tractarian, announced his long-suspected conversion to Roman Catholicism.[75]

Tractarianism, however, had already impeded intellectual life in Oxford: Pattison wrote that 'It [the decline of Tractarianism] was a deliverance from the nightmare which had oppressed Oxford for fifteen years ... Probably there was no period of our history during which ... the ordinary study of the classics was so profitless or at so low an ebb as during the period of the tractarian controversy.'[76] It also splintered the forces of reform, allowing conservatives who opposed both sides of the Oriel Fellowship more room for manoeuvre. (A story went around that when a dog had bitten Benjamin Jowett, the University's leading reformer and later Master of Balliol, Jowett had it expelled from Balliol but Hawkins, a former student at St John's and at that

---

73 Quoted in Faught (2004) p. 8.
74 Tuckwell (1909) p. 80.
75 The Martyrs' Memorial, built to commemorate the three Protestant bishops burnt in 1555, was an early attempt to flush out crypto-Catholics among the Tractarians by seeing if they would donate to it or not (Faught, 2004, p. 90).
76 Pattison (1885) pp. 236–7.

time Oriel's Provost, 'received the animal and tenderly entertained it'.[77])

For all their limitations and divisions, however, the reformers had done enough to prepare the ground. In 1850, after a petition from graduates and the Royal Society, the government established commissions to investigate the Universities of Oxford and Cambridge; reformers were ready to take full advantage and drag *all* the colleges, kicking and screaming if necessary, into the modern age. In part the impetus was a recognition of the success of the professorial, German model of the university: based on the state's aims rather than giving power to individual academics, it was producing most of the interesting research in Europe at the time. The commissioners therefore came to Oxford and began examining college statutes (often a difficult task, as there were few copies in existence and the colleges would frequently refuse to hand them over) and finances (an almost impossible task as no Oxford college provided financial information) with a view to turning the University into a modern institution for teaching and research.[78] Fellowships and scholarships were opened up; finances were redirected towards the support of new professors who would drive research forward in the University; the need for Fellows to take holy orders and for undergraduates to be Anglicans was removed. (The requirement that Fellows and those taking higher degrees be Anglicans would go in 1871.)

St John's held out until the bitter end, sending proposals and counter-proposals to increasingly frustrated commissioners. Did the College really have to break its link with the Merchant Taylors' School, which sent it so many good scholars? Must they really stop accepting the Founder's kin? Must the Fellowships

---

77 Tuckwell (1909) p. 161.
78 Neild (2012) p. 7.

be thrown open to the most qualified men, rather than those linked to the College? In the end the College was the very last in Oxford to be reformed (and although most of the Fellowships *were* thrown open, in 1853 St John's accepted a donation from the will of Dudley Fereday which established four Fellowships for, in the first instance, relatives of the donor and, in the second, natives of Staffordshire).

The changes would, in the fullness of time, make a dramatic difference. In the short term, however, it gave St John's a new purpose: it became the home of resistance against further reform; or, as the conservatives preferred to term it, 'Progress falsely so-called'.[79]

A College Unsuccessfully Reformed

Change is rarely perfect, and so there are always excuses for those sceptical of it. Some reformers like Mark Pattison thought that the University should follow Germany's lead and be focused on research. As a result he became 'a sort of troglodyte and was practically invisible to the ordinary member of the University'.[80] He was also caricatured by George Eliot, who preferred Jowett's teaching-focused party, as the pedant Casaubon in *Middlemarch*. But the criticism was not all on one side. Jowett's focus on impacting the world through his graduates meant many Oxonians 'regarded Dr. Jowett as less of a scholar than he fancied himself to be, a ruthless seeker after notoriety for himself and his college, a cultivator of the great, and a deliberate *poseur*'.[81]

Religious criticism turned to mockery: in *The New Republic*

---

79 Oman (1941) pp. viii–ix.
80 Ibid. p. 210.
81 Ibid. p. 209.

Intellectual Capital

Dr Jenkinson, a character transparently based on Jowett, reads from the Koran and gives a sermon:

> '– And now –' (at the sound of this word the whole congregation rose automatically to their feet), 'I will ask you,' the Doctor went on after a pause, 'to conclude this morning's service by doing what I trust I have shown that all here may sincerely and honestly do. I mean, I will ask you to recite after me the Apostles' Creed.' This appeal took the whole congregation quite aback.[82]

As one of them noted, 'Dr. Jenkinson's Christianity is really a new firm trading under an old name, and trying to purchase the goodwill of the former establishment.'[83]

Faced with a divided foe, the conservatives could tell themselves they were just pointing out the excesses of those seeking a nebulous 'Wider Oneness', maintaining religious propriety, and ensuring all scholarship was up to scratch.[84] In reality however an opportunity to change was being wasted. Standards at St John's, and other colleges like it, did gradually improve with those of the University as the open Fellowships resulted in new blood, but change was not happening as fast as it could have done.

While St John's may not have been seeing that much academic growth, its fiscal health was looking more promising – and all because of the short Act mentioned at the start of the chapter. The College's investments in 1855 were much the same as they had been just after its foundation, and the accounts reflect this. Each year the bursar drew up the *Computus Annus*,

---

82 Mallock (1906) p. 119.
83 Ibid. p. 123.
84 Oman (1941) p. 209.

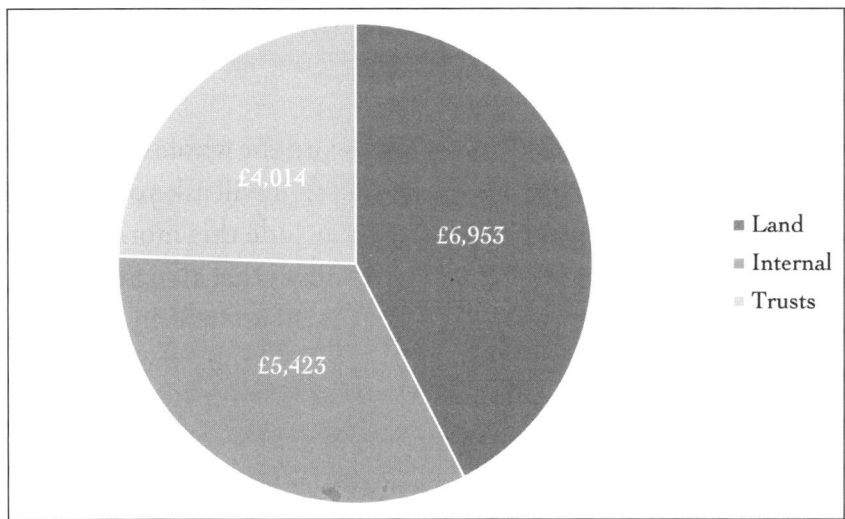

Figure 1.1: St John's Sources of Income, 1855

a long book which changed little in format over the centuries. Income and spending were listed by source: so payments from tenants were not split into agricultural, residential, commercial, etc. but into whether the payment was regular, casual (for example heriots – a form of death duty levied on tenants of copyhold property, a quasi-feudal structure where the lord of the manor still was owed customary duties), a quit rent (another feudal relic, paid to exempt the tenant from obligations), etc. Charmingly there is a column entitled *Reditus ex Ovibus*: literally 'returns from the sheep'. By 1855 these woolly patrons were contributing £15 annually to scholarship.[85]

Income came from three major sources: internal payments (such as for food, rent and tuition); investment income from land; and income from various trusts.[86] These trusts were

---

85 SJC ACC I.A.204.
86 SJC ACC I.A.204. Note that another significant item on the income side is

typically invested in land as well – the most important was Richard Rawlinson's bequest, which accounted for just over half of the College's trust income and mainly consisted of rents from the estate of Wasperton. Unlike the other two sources, much of the income from the trusts was restricted to spending on specified purposes such as the chapel (although some trusts existed to augment the income of particular Fellows, which would have allowed College income to be spent on other ends, even if that is not what the donor had envisaged).

Such a heavy investment in land was not unusual at the time – in fact for a perpetual institution like an Oxford college, it was the only investment option available. (The Universities and Colleges Estates Act 1858 enabled colleges to invest in government securities as well.) As bodies with a charitable purpose, they were forbidden from doing anything considered too risky – the worry was that one generation of Fellows would act to enrich themselves at the expense of their successors – and so the company shares in which rich individuals were increasingly investing (or speculating) were off limits, at least for their permanent endowments. 'Land' encompasses housing property, but at this point much of the College's wealth was in farmland.[87]

Owning land, however, was not just about getting an

---

debts owed to the College – in 1855 these were £5,731. Against these we have debts which the College owed of £5,839, and such figures are typical for the period. Some of the income received in 1855, therefore, probably reflects income that should have been paid in previous years, which will roughly offset the income it should have received in 1855, but did not.

87 It is difficult to tell exactly how much, but in 1881 just 32 per cent of the College's income from estates was coming from housing and related sources, and much of this is attributable to North Oxford. In 1855, when all that development was still to come, perhaps 10 per cent of the College's estates income was from housing (SJC ACC I.B.2).

investment return. The great aristocratic families typically had 'broad acres' and a social cachet was attached: the owner was intimately involved in the lives of the people who lived on his estate. Land was not merely a commodity to trade and maximise investment returns from. The connection was even stronger if the landowner also owned the 'advowson': the right to nominate the priest for the parish. Like other colleges, St John's owned several of these as they were a natural destination for those of its Fellows who did not want to continue the academic life. Being (quite literally) lord of the manor, with responsibility for the souls of the inhabitants, meant that trading land away or maximising investment returns were foreign ideas to the Fellowship.

Income generation from land had improved – albeit very gradually – over the centuries. In the eighteenth century it seems to have been common for colleges not to go to the trouble of actually visiting their far-flung farms and collecting their rents: instead they sold the right to collect the rents to a specialist. The difference between what the specialist paid and what they collected was their compensation, but this could easily be excessive, as payments were commonly 'in kind' and so depended on the quality of the farm and farmer, which the specialist probably knew better than the college. Merton College seems to have fallen foul of a particularly sharp operator called Ralph Carr, who has been estimated to have made a return on his spending of between 200 and 300 per cent.[88] By the beginning of the nineteenth century Merton was more cautious.

Income from farmland was still mainly from 'beneficial leases': a form of tenure where the farmer would pay the College a nominal annual rent but a large 'fine' every seven years to renew the lease (confusingly for twenty-one years – after seven years

---

88 Purdue (1997) p. 12.

they would renew again, so a lease with fourteen years to run would be reset to twenty-one years). The farmer was responsible for investing in the farm and because the arrangement might last indefinitely they had an incentive to do so. The College spent relatively little on managing its investment, but at the cost of irregular payments and, more importantly, not getting the maximum rent possible from its farms. By the beginning of the nineteenth century 'rack renting' – charging an annual rent, based on the market value of the land, and taking responsibility for investments in it – was the hottest trend around, and every progressive college was thinking about how they could implement it.

Given the incentives for investment and lower management fees, why were beneficial leases less financially attractive to colleges than rack renting? First, although receiving income every seven years wasn't ideal for a college, the large upfront payment was even less ideal for a farmer. Annual payments meant landlords were no longer requiring farmers to effectively loan them money, and didn't have to compensate them for this. Similarly, tenants on beneficial leases were exposed to fluctuations in the real value of the farmland. By charging an annual adjustable rent, landlords effectively provided insurance to tenants by taking the risk on themselves, although in practice the tenants, who could not easily move, seem to have borne more risk from the landlord *not* adjusting the rent.[89] Furthermore, given enough information about best practice in farming, the College was potentially better placed to invest in improvements than the tenant.

Most significant, however, was the fact that the fines were

---

89 Such 'insurance' works by the landlord adjusting the rents in line with the realised market value; in practice these adjustments could lag behind changes in conditions (Offer, 1991, p. 117).

well below the market value, simply because *they always had been*. The fine was set by working out the appropriate annual rent for the property and then multiplying it, and this multiple was astonishingly low: typically between 1.25 and 1.5, although towards the end of the eighteenth century it sometimes reached 2.[90] In theory landowners could increase the multiple, but doing so led to resistance: when Queen's College made such an attempt in 1735 the tenants were so outraged that they persuaded the House of Commons to vote on it (although the MPs ended up supporting Queen's).[91] Because it was a new type of economic relationship, charging a rack rent seems to have allowed landowners to evade these critiques.

Such an explanation runs counter to an economist's intuition, although perhaps not that of the average person. But as bodies with a social purpose, colleges may have felt it was inappropriate to squeeze as much as possible from tenants. And as we saw with Merton, there definitely were occasions when colleges would collect less than, with a little due diligence, they could have done.

The snag was that transforming the tenancies into rack rents meant running the leases out and thus forgoing the fines for fourteen years. Colleges were historically restricted from borrowing to fund the shortfall and so had to sacrifice short-term income for a long-term benefit.[92] But in time the case for

---

90 Dunbabin (1986) p. 277.
91 Ibid. p. 279.
92 Although not all of them seem to have scrupulously followed the law. All Souls 'borrowed' from its Penh Trust Estate, which existed to support poor clergymen – as a later bursar noted, this was 'perhaps an improper, but certainly a helpful, expedient' (Faber, 1950, p. 52). Tuckwell claims that Copleston borrowed to smooth the transition at Oriel, it is possible that the same expedient was used (Tuckwell, 1909, p. 31).

doing this became overwhelming: in 1872 Magdalen College received just under £7,000 from lands on beneficial leases which could have brought in over £23,000 had they been rack rented (although this does not account for the management costs that would have resulted). It was giving up another £8,000 on houses on beneficial leases.[93] This discrepancy had already led it to stop renewing beneficial leases in 1864.[94] St John's was doing even worse, getting just 23 per cent of the theoretical rack rent on its beneficial leases.[95] It also seems that tenants had not invested as much as they might have done, preferring stable fines, so there had been a missed opportunity to improve the land.[96] The colleges accordingly pushed ahead with turning their beneficial leases into rack rents, albeit at different paces: Balliol was beginning in the 1750s, and in the early nineteenth century Edward Copleston, at the time Oriel's bursar, stopped renewing all its leases and was reputed to have tripled the College's income.[97] In 1860 the Universities and College Estates Act was extended and colleges were allowed to raise loans to smooth the transition, after which even the laggards began to make a serious effort to modernise.[98] St John's seems to have really started making a dent in its beneficial leases at this point.[99]

The whole process then went into reverse when the

---

93 Universities Commission (1874) p. 86.
94 Ibid. p. 89.
95 Ibid. p. 109. The Commissioners claim that it was getting only 4 per cent of the potential rack rent value on its houses on beneficial leases, but it seems that there must have been some confusion with long-lease property here, despite this being listed separately.
96 Turner (2000) p. 22.
97 Darwall-Smith (2008) p. 323; Tuckwell (1909) p. 31.
98 Dunbabin (1997) pp. 385–6.
99 Hinchcliffe (1992) p. 7.

Agricultural Depression hit in the 1870s.[100] The removal of tariffs on imports of agricultural products in 1846 meant that British farmers now received the world price (more or less) for their grain. The United States was beginning to expand into the vast plains of the Midwest, and new land began to be cultivated. Combined with a reduction in the cost of transporting grain around the world owing to new railways and better ships, this resulted in additional supply which pushed prices down in Britain. The fact that so much land had become rack rented made the situation worse. The colleges' experiences paralleled those of banks in the Great Recession. They may have owned many different and geographically dispersed farms, just as the banks were exposed to mortgages from many different regions of the US. But an economic hit to agriculture, just like a hit to the housing market, affected all of them. The insurance they had effectively provided to tenants was now having to be paid, and what made sense for many small, independent transactions did not make sense for what was effectively a single, large transaction.

The Fellowship was concerned: after dinner in the Senior Common Room, Henry Jardine Bidder (the College's 'Keeper of the Groves' and creator of its famous Alpine rockery) recorded in the Fellows' Bet Book 'Bidder bets Goodrick a bottle of Chateau d'Yquem that before the end of 1890 wheat will have been quoted at 40/- for four consecutive weeks.'[101] This price influenced how much money the College could expect to get in rent from its farms when the rates came up to be renewed. Other colleges also suffered: from 1883 (when reliable records begin)

---

100 British agriculture had been struggling before that, but based on indexes of wheat and food prices Fletcher argues that it was 1876 when things really took a turn for the worse, and 1896 when they improved (Fletcher, 1961, pp. 417–18).
101 SJC SCR B.11.

to 1896, University College's external revenues had dropped 11 per cent and Corpus Christi's 30 per cent. Trinity's had dropped 16 per cent. In contrast, St John's were up 10 per cent. What was going on?

The answer comes back to the short Act of Parliament mentioned at the beginning of the chapter. Like other colleges, St John's *had* taken a hit on its agricultural portfolio: revenues from farms had fallen 22 per cent.[102] But it had more than made up for the loss by increasing its external revenues from another type of asset class: housing. This revenue had increased by 61 per cent (although that figure does not account for the increased spending in which the College had engaged to finance the increase), and the growth disproportionately came from building in North Oxford.[103]

Building for Success

The fields north of the College had finally become ripe for building as the city of Oxford expanded. Bounded to the west by Port Meadow – beautiful open grassland that regularly flooded and so was unsuitable for building on – and to the east by the Cherwell river, the space was just waiting to be turned into suburban housing. In *North Oxford* Tanis Hinchcliffe explodes the myth that the suburb's creation was only about dons being allowed to marry and moving out of their colleges to have families: heads of households in the 'professions' were only 37.9 per cent of the residents in the central area of North Oxford in 1881.[104] 'Private Income' formed another 31.2 per cent: it was a solidly

---
102 Data from University of Oxford (1883, 1896): I.(1), I.(2), I.(10).
103 Ibid.: I.(3), I.(4), I.(5).
104 Hinchcliffe (1992) p. 168.

middle-class area. The western part of the estate was dominated by artisans or people working in trades, and the College dictated that many of the cottages in the west were designed so that they would be affordable for this group.[105]

From a financial perspective, the suburb's creation is characterised by risk aversion. The College followed what had become the typical playbook for an institution with building land: lease plots to builder-developers (who would often subcontract them to other builders) but include covenants governing what could be built and how the buildings were to be managed after people moved in. As was standard, these were 99-year 'long leases'. The College avoided risk by having the developer spend the money to build the house and take on the job of selling a sub-lease on it to the eventual tenant; the developer's payoff came from the spread between the (very low) rent they paid the College and the rent they could get from a tenant. At the end of the ninety-nine years, the whole plot – land and house – would revert to the College's ownership.

None of this was out of the ordinary. Great families, often with estates in London, had been following such an approach for centuries and were well into the cycle of regaining possession and re-leasing. They used exactly the same kind of risk-shifting: as Edward Ryde, a former President of the Surveyors' Institution, told the Select Committee on Town Holdings, 'No freeholder would undertake a building operation which, after all, is the most risky operation you can undertake. It is a most capricious thing. You think building land is as ripe as possible, and to all appearances it is, and presently you build upon it, but no tenant comes, and there it remains a howling wilderness for

---

105 Hinchcliffe (1992) pp. 84, 171.

years to come.'[106] Other colleges had carried out this form of development before St John's: Magdalen was granted a Private Act to offer building leases for its land in Southwark in 1777.[107] And having got its own Act, St John's was not in a rush: the suburb crept northwards towards Summertown, but would only arrive there in 1914.[108] The College's strategy was to offer building plots only when it was sure there would be demand for them (if possible, the College wanted plots to be taken by someone who intended to live in the home they were building, guaranteeing the demand). This reduced the finance the College had to raise to fund the sewers and roads which went along with the new development.

But the College's caution in expanding was not excessive. Indeed, it was partially informed by the experience of Park Town. This development was one of the few areas in North Oxford it did not own, and was built before the tide of St John's building plots washed around it. It was not a financial success: the development company was liquidated in 1861, just four years after it had been set up, owing to insufficient demand for the houses.[109] Furthermore, while the College was following a conservative path, it was far from being Britain's least enthusiastic institutional developer. When Eton College had considered turning its Chalcots Estate in North London into a building development, it held off because the Fellows treated the fines from the beneficial leases as non-standard income and so distributed them among themselves.[110] Regular rents, on the other

---

[106] Quoted in Anderson (2009) p. 74.
[107] Brockliss (2008) p. 368.
[108] Hinchcliffe (1992) p. 189.
[109] Ibid. p. 33.
[110] Dowling (1997) p. 20.

hand, went into the school's general budget. Chalcots was only developed once a mortgage had been raised to compensate the Fellows for their loss.[111] All Souls was even worse – they eventually got round to developing their lands in Middlesex only after their dedicated surveyor, J. J. Done, persuaded them to do so in 1888. (He had been trying for over a decade, but the College had rejected his proposals in 1877 and 1884.[112])

Amid this field St John's does not stand out as particularly adventurous or particularly conservative. Taking unspoiled fields and building on them had become commonplace enough that Gilbert and Sullivan satirised it in *Patience*. The 'fleshly poet', Bunthorne, admits that his aestheticism is an act: 'between you and me, I don't like poetry. It's hollow, unsubstantial – unsatisfactory. What's the use of yearning for Elysian Fields when you know you can't get 'em, and would only let 'em out on building leases if you had 'em?'[113] The College saw a fairly obvious opportunity and took advantage of it in the standard, sensible way. And, as we have seen, their finances prospered as a result.

Twentieth-Century Transformation?

All the College's money had not transformed it into a leading institution of education within Oxford. To think that it might do so is, in some senses, to miss the point. It is true that other colleges were reforming themselves and improving teaching, or supporting research; but colleges were independent and nothing meant that St John's had to follow their lead – or even recognise it to be a lead. At a College increasingly dedicated to resisting

---

111 EC COLL/CHAL/1/3/2/8 p. 15.
112 Faber (1950) p. 60.
113 Gilbert and Sullivan (1881) p. 11.

the changes going on elsewhere in the University, putting serious thought into how to copy even benign innovations would have seemed subversive. So standards remained low, as the case of Charles Yates Fell illustrates.

Charles came up in 1867 and entered the relatively new Final Honour School of Law and History.[114] Just entering for an honour school was a good sign – many of his contemporaries were still happy to get the much less rigorous pass degree. But why not the more prestigious Literae Humaniores (Classics)? Charles's Greek, unfortunately, wasn't up to it. And not – or so he assures us – because of his own failings: 'I was full of work and eager enough and only wanted proper directions, but I rarely got any help or direction at all.' The academic level was not high, with tutors and students alike focused on getting drunk: 'temperance was unheard of and the wine and beer that was daily put away seems now idiotic and worse'. He worked 'very hard, but without the least idea how, and with no one to show me'. He blamed his school for not teaching him how to learn, and looked on enviously at the men from Merchant Taylors', who were reading for Greats – albeit with the help of out-of-College 'coaches' (which is probably how the other two candidates from St John's that year got their First and Second). Poor Charles received a Third, and felt that, given the limitations he laboured under, he could hardly have done better. A friendly Fellow called Richard Clarke wrote to his father separately, supporting the young man's claims that he never stood much of a chance. Clarke later wrote a serious treatise on logic, and perhaps could have reformed teaching in the College – had he not been thrown out for converting to Catholicism two years after Charles graduated.

---

114 Charles's story is told in the *College Record* (1978) pp. 28–31.

Figure 1.2: Proportional Spending on Tuition

Standards began to improve when a remarkable Fellow named Sidney Ball joined the College in 1882. Ball, with his undergraduate degree from Oriel and socialist beliefs, certainly did not consider progress to be 'falsely so called'. He set about reforming St John's, becoming Senior Tutor (responsible for overseeing undergraduate education) in 1885. Under his leadership, students could expect to be invited to reading parties in the vacations, or engaged in political and ethical discussion late into the night. Not content with changing St John's, he was prominent in setting up societies to reform the University, and for that reason attracted widespread notoriety. As one student wrote, 'there has been no conspiracy in Oxford against time-worn traditions and opinions in which he has not been concerned.'[115] One example was advocating against compulsory chapel – despite Ball himself being an avid church-goer.

---

115 Ball (1923) p. 77.

By the end of ultra-conservative James Bellamy's presidency Ball was essentially running the College on the older man's behalf, and had won his confidence despite his political views. His success can be summarised in his own words: 'I have seen my own College raised from a Pass to an Honours College … it has become increasingly difficult for a rich man to come up [to Oxford generally] … simply in order to "have a good time".'[116] In part this must have come down to his ability to persuade the College to commit more money: throughout his tenure the tuition fund exceeded tuition fees by about 15 per cent, but spending as a proportion of total income rose from around 8 per cent to 13 per cent.

Such worthy work did not go unchallenged. When Ball received his Fellowship his old headmaster wrote to congratulate him, but also to offer some advice: 'Don't stay too long at St. John's. Somehow the Fellows there go off their heads after awhile, or something exceedingly like it. But let us hope you are the beginning of a new order.'[117] Experience proved this to be true. When Ball had the temerity to get married – something allowed under the new statutes, but very much not the done thing – the College used a technical device to strip him of his Fellowship (while keeping him as Senior Tutor). Ball considered it 'a very unworthy dodge, to put it mildly … there can be no doubt that the College has no moral ground to stand upon.'[118] He also had to move out of his beloved rooms, as Bellamy said he 'wasn't going to have Mrs. Ball trundling her perambulator in

---

116 Ball (1923) p. 107.
117 Ibid. p. 39.
118 Ibid. p. 50. The Statutes allowed a Fellow to marry after seven years, but the College cancelled Ball's Fellowship and re-elected him to one so that he had technically been a Fellow for just one year concurrently, rather than eight.

the quad'.[119] His Fellowship was eventually reinstated, presumably after the ritual humiliation had been judged to have served its purpose. But this was not all. When Bellamy did retire, Ball seemed a natural choice to be the next President, but a conservative faction of Fellows were disquieted by his radical politics and backed Hutton, the College historian. In the event a compromise candidate – Herbert Armitage James, then headmaster of Rugby – was elected, on the grounds that he would probably retire or die fairly soon and by then the balance of power might have shifted enough that one side could win. Instead James outlived both candidates.[120]

Meanwhile the College was recovering from financial pressures. Although North Oxford was bringing in increasing amounts of income, the agricultural depression was biting St John's as well, and it was regularly running a deficit. Bellamy had already had to stand between the Fellows and financial pain, paying the 22 per cent of their salaries which the College was unable to provide.[121] This was a very considerable donation and doubtless deeply appreciated, although Bellamy could certainly afford it: at death his estate had a net value of £233,778, equivalent to over £23m at the time of publication.[122] The situation was worsened by the state of the Bursary. The College had only introduced a modern system of accounting after the University made it do so, and the auditor lamented that the College had neither a ledger of loans nor a register of properties.[123] Key individuals were personally responsible for gathering and holding

---

119 Ball (1923) p. 62.
120 Mabbott (1986) p. 43.
121 SJC ADM III.D.1 (1889 Report).
122 High Court of Justice (21 Dec. 1909).
123 SJC ADM III.D.1 (1883 Report).

large amounts of money. In such a chaotic situation it was not difficult to commit fraud, and on at least two occasions it did occur: in 1889 the bailiff, who was collecting rents from the College's farms, ran off with over £3,565.[124] Accepting responsibility, the bursar, T. S. Omond, resigned.[125] Unfortunately his replacement, W. J. W. Glasson, also stole £1,558 from the College in 1896 – the College accounts record the debt being written off against his name.[126]

Afterwards the situation began to improve, both financially and administratively, and by the start of the First World War the College was running a surplus of over £5,000.[127] Or so it seemed – but after the war recriminations would begin anew, with the bursar writing to the President to alert him to the fact that financial reports might as well 'have been dispensed with altogether, as they fail entirely to indicate the dangerous point to which the Expenditure of the College compared with receipts is heading'.[128] St John's was not floating enough money to meet its commitments, and had taken on more than £9,000 in unauthorised loans. Slowly – not least owing to the dogged efforts of the new bursar, R. V. O. Hart-Synnot – the College was once again put on a sounder financial footing.

Oxford, too, was changing. Surprisingly this can be seen in perhaps the most famous Oxford novel, Evelyn Waugh's *Brideshead Revisited*. The book is often remembered as a celebration of Oxonian decadence (although the early reference to Poussin's *Et in Arcadia Ego*, which shows death and corruption in

---

124 SJC ADM III.D.1 (1889 Report).
125 In fact he had been planning to resign even before the theft occurred (Hinchcliffe, 1992, p. 76).
126 University of Oxford (1896) Balance Sheet.
127 SJC ADM III.D.1 (1914 Report).
128 SJC ADM III.D.1 (1919 Report).

an apparent idyll, should make us question this simplistic interpretation) but in fact it indicates a remarkable climbdown for its author.[129] Growing up, Waugh had enjoyed reading Beverley Nichols' *Patchwork* – a rather bad novel about a man who, traumatised by serving in the First World War, goes up to a profoundly changed Oxford and sets about recreating the pre-war culture.[130] Although he is successful tragedy strikes at the end and, the iron having entered his soul, he leaves for New York, albeit with a timeless Oxford still in his mind. The parallel to the sudden turn in Waugh's *Vile Bodies* – where even the language suddenly becomes harder and more visceral in the final moment – is striking. Both *Vile Bodies* and *Patchwork* are, at least in part, a celebration of attempts to recreate what the First World War had destroyed, and in his memoirs Waugh claims to have experienced this too: 'all the time it seemed to me that there was a quintessential Oxford … It is not given to all her sons either to seek or find this secret, but it was very near the surface in 1922.'[131]

Yet when he came to write *Brideshead* we see, perhaps unconsciously, a different emphasis. Many of its most sumptuous scenes occur outside Oxford; to a significant degree the University is obscured rather than revealed. It is the country house of Brideshead, not the dreaming spires, which forms the spiritual centre of the novel. The world of little work and widespread leisure (Waugh himself went down before finishing his degree after losing his scholarship for poor examination performance)

---

129 Poussin's paintings (one in Chatsworth House and one in the Louvre, both of which Waugh could have seen) seem the most likely source of inspiration, although he was not the only painter to produce such works.
130 Waugh (1983) p. 167.
131 Ibid. p. 167.

was passing away, as Waugh himself – indeed, despite himself – notes at length in his memoirs.[132] A new kind of student was becoming ascendent: as one of the dons recalled, 'They seem positively to thirst for knowledge and scribble away in their note-books like lunatics. I can't remember a single instance of such stern endeavour in pre-war days.'[133]

And so it continued. The financial situation kept on improving, with better management of the College farms leading to higher returns. The contributions from the long leases on the North Oxford houses were less than they might have been: because the rents were fixed they were eroded by rising prices, which had not been considered a problem in the mid-nineteenth century but proved to be one when inflation soared after the First World War. Still, they provided the great hope for the College's financial future, because the leases would, from the 1950s, start falling in – the College would receive the land and houses back, to do with as they wished. Even the Second World War did not put a serious dent in the College's prosperity. Rationing did have an effect, of course, but in an attenuated form: the Steward of the Senior Common Room was most worried about the port shortage it caused.[134] Everything was looking rosy.

A Glowing SCR and Growing Property Problem

By the 1950s St John's still didn't cut much of a figure in the

---

132 Waugh (1983) pp. 169–71. Interestingly, he also writes that one of his closest friends, 'Hamish Lennox', 'soon went down to take a course in architecture in London; but he continued to haunt Oxford and for two or three years we were inseparable ... During Hamish's visits to Oxford we saw little of the university, spending our days driving in his motor round the surrounding villages' (pp. 192–3).
133 G. N. Clark quoted in Graves (1960) p. 238.
134 Mabbott (1986) p. 115.

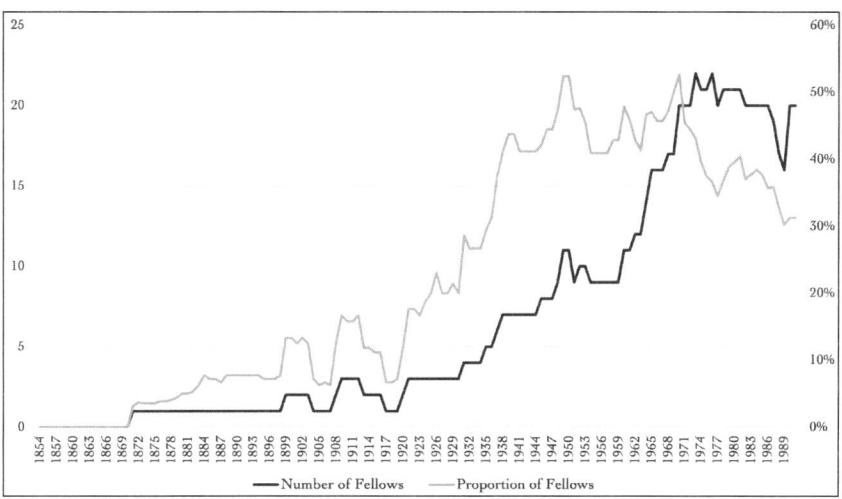

Figure 1.3: Members of the Fellowship who would become Fellows of the British Academy or Royal Society

University. Students themselves don't seem to have had a very high opinion of the place. Harvey Pitcher (m. 1957) noted that St John's seemed to him 'a very average middle-of-the-road sort of College, perfectly respectable but not very exciting. It did not, so far as I recall, have a reputation for excellence in any particular area.'[135] In *Oxford: The Novel*, A. D. Harvey's (m. 1966) protagonist states, 'Anyway St. John's was generally said to be full of ... people who had failed to get into Balliol.'[136]

---

135 Private correspondence.
136 Bellingham (1981) p. 12. In private correspondence, Harvey emphasised that this was 'a typical flip undergraduate remark ... Generally speaking I think the college was regarded as rather average.' Harvey's story is interesting: after reading History at St John's he went to Cambridge for his doctorate, hoping to become a novelist. He went on to publish several works of history but, more notably, many works under pseudonymous names, including reviews of unwritten works of literature credited to still other pseudonyms. Most notably, he published a short piece in *The Dickensian*

Intellectual Capital

On the other hand, the Fellowship was improving. It is always difficult to establish how good a body of academics are – not least because aims such as teaching and research are distinct, and often in conflict – but we do have some clues. If we look at the proportion of Fellows who would go on to become Fellows of the Royal Society or British Academy then we see that the 1950s were a high point for the Senior Common Room. Furthermore, the Fellowship was a sign of a more open College – although many Fellows still had an Oxford background, few now came from St John's itself, which was a historic shift. The younger Fellows showed their mettle by declining to appoint Edward Maufe, the College's architect (and an alumnus), to build a new range in North Quad which would have completed the quadrangle in much the same style as the existing ranges. Instead a radical hexagonal cluster, called the Beehive, was constructed as an accommodation block. This was not a completely modern design – the building was not made of concrete but rather of expensive Portland stone which *looked* like concrete; the initial proposal to have corridors was shot down on the grounds that only women's colleges (and Keble) had corridors rather than staircases – but it was a striking change, and remains an eyesore to this day.

Why did this improvement in the quality of Fellows not translate into improved teaching? Fellows did, it seems, care about the quality of their students – but they also had other aims. Bill Hayes, a physicist who became a Fellow in 1960, was

---

inventing a meeting between Dickens and Dostoevsky. When this was challenged as suspicious, the academic Eric Naiman investigated, eventually tracing the entire assemblage back to Harvey by recognising a passage from *Oxford: The Novel* (itself published both under Harvey's real name and later under the pseudonym Leo Bellingham) which Harvey had reused. He wrote up the entire story, which is well worth a read, for the *Times Literary Supplement*.

forced to have a serious fight with Harold Thompson, the Chemistry Fellow (and a man of significant academic distinction) over Engineering admissions. Thompson was committed to getting first-class chemists admitted to the College. On the other hand, he had been rather less concerned about the quality of engineers and 'regarded engineering as a route into the College for promising footballers'.[137] These practices were not unique to St John's: around the same time a tutor at Keble made it his mission to recruit the Eton rowing VIII, no matter how undistinguished academically they might be ('his strategy was remarkably successful, if accumulating Etonian oarsmen can be accounted success'); and as late as 1975 the Principal of St Edmund Hall is alleged to have attempted to strike a deal with Westminster, whereby they would take 'borderline cases' if Westminster occasionally sent someone really good.[138]

Even when it came to teaching, however, things were beginning to change. Much of the credit must go to Keith Thomas, a History Fellow who joined the College from All Souls in 1957. Contemporaries noticed that this very young and intimidatingly well-read man was something new – excellent at research and a fantastic tutor, soon bringing the College a clutch of Firsts in History.[139] Similarly, the appointment of John Carey (who had read English at St John's and then joined Keble) and John White (a chemist) in 1964 led to a significant uplift in the quality of tuition. But progress was uneven, in part because there was no central figure driving up standards throughout the College. Instead a few subjects reformed, driven by their individual tutors. Even here there was countervailing pressure: Thomas

---

137 Bill Hayes' private memoirs.
138 Carey (2015) p. 175, Rae (2009) p. 77.
139 Private correspondence.

recalls being hauled into the Presidential Lodgings to receive a dressing-down from President William Costin (himself a constitutional historian). St John's historians, he was told, were getting too many Firsts: 'We're not Balliol! St John's has always turned out middle-ranking civil servants and we should continue to do so.' (Ironically, in the preface to his history of St John's, Costin claimed that the common thread throughout the College's history was 'an abiding love of learning'.)[140] Thus the College entered the mid-1960s with a distinguished Fellowship but a generally unremarkable student body.

Perhaps the Fellows were distracted. Oxford was changing, and for a university which has too often seen change as anathema, predicting where battle would be joined was an important task. The root of the problem was that the University was growing, not least due to expansion after the Second World War, with many more students having the means to come to Oxford thanks to local authority grants. This put pressure on the traditional model of students living in college throughout their degrees: St John's certainly did not have enough space, despite constructing the Beehive, and many students 'lived out' in approved lodgings. The rest of the city was growing as well, and traffic congestion was getting worse. The city council responded by developing a town plan and was proposing building relief roads through Christ Church Meadow and the historic Lamb & Flag pub, directly north of St John's. Understandably, there was significant opposition.

The uncertainty also made it harder to decide what to do about the long leases, which were starting to fall in. Much of North Oxford was no longer in good repair, which was not uncommon for leasehold houses, especially when they were

---

140 Costin (1958) p. v.

sub-let towards the end of the lease. In theory whoever held the lease when it fell in was liable for 'dilapidations': payments to return the building to the state it was in when it was built. But often it was not possible to get such payments from departing tenants. In the nineteenth century St John's kept a notebook of dilapidations, and we see that many minor payments from tenants were received throughout their tenancies.[141] By the mid-twentieth century, however, the College faced 'what seems to be a losing battle for dilapidation money from penniless lessees'.[142] Redevelopment was therefore necessary but would be expensive – too expensive for the College to fund on its own. And just like the original building of North Oxford, it would require urban and financial planning. But such planning was the very thing frustrated by the uncertainty about the town plan.

St John's faced pressure from another direction too, in the person of Lord Harcourt. A graduate of Christ Church, he was mainly interested in St John's through his role as chairman of the Oxford Preservation Trust. The Trust had one major goal – to protect Oxford's beautiful, historic architecture – and one major problem – the city clearly needed to grow so people had somewhere to live, but fitting more people in the centre would necessarily require redevelopment and destruction. Meanwhile the city's 'base and brickish skirt' of suburbs had already smothered many pleasant fields and meadows, and no one really wanted it to spread further. The obvious solution was higher density housing outside the centre but in an area which was already built up. Like North Oxford.

Faced with this challenging set of circumstances and competing interests, the College did what Oxford colleges do best:

---

141 SJC MUN V.C.49.
142 SJC MUN V.C.66.

it delayed.[143] Feelers were sent out to the city council to protest against the new roads (with eventual success). As the 1950s wore on, however, and more leases fell in, the question of what to do became ever more pressing. In 1959, Arthur Garrard, the bursar, began conversations with a company called Townmaker about redeveloping Walton Manor, in the heart of the North Oxford Estate, as a village within a suburb.[144]

Today, those plans look absolutely astonishing. An architect named Lionel Brett was asked to survey the area and suggest options. He came back with a plan to bulldoze the corner of Leckford and Woodstock Road and build 'a row of four-storey flats, and, behind them, an 18-storey tower block of flats'.[145] It is hard to believe that anyone could seriously have expected the College to be able to get away with building what would undoubtedly have been an eyesore in the leafy suburb, ruining Oxford's famous skyline in the process. And yet the council's planning officer was supportive: 'With the building of an 18-storey tower of flats he expressed entire agreement and implied that the Planning Committee was already being "conditioned" to the idea that such buildings, properly sited, were the logical solution to the problem of how to increase a population within an unexpandable boundary.'[146] And in 1963 the Engineering Department opened its Thom Building, perhaps the ugliest thing in Oxford today: a hulking mass of glass and concrete, polluting views from Port Meadow since its construction. Nonetheless, even if the council was willing to wave it through, local opposition would probably have put an end to the outrageous plan for Walton Manor.

---

143 SJC ADM II.C.1.
144 SJC ADM II.C.2.
145 Ibid.
146 Ibid.

To fund the development the College planned to sell other parts of the estate. The plan received further impetus when the College's first Fellow in Economics, George Richardson, submitted a note to the finance committee worrying about their exposure to North Oxford.[147] He pointed out that 70 per cent of the College's net income was from houses, either on rack rents or long leases, and most of these were in North Oxford. A diverse portfolio was safer than putting all your eggs in one basket. Furthermore, in an age of inflation long leases weren't a very suitable asset for a long-term investor like the College to hold anyway. Finally, he raised the spectre of political risk: the Labour Party had promised to reintroduce rent control if they got into power, which would severely limit the returns from most of the College's portfolio. In contrast equities, which formed just 1.2 per cent of the portfolio by net income, 'have much to commend them from the point of view of the institutional investor. They permit risk spreading, for the income from a diversified holding will not depend on the prosperity of particular industries or localities.' Although colleges had historically been prohibited from investing in them (at least with endowed capital – I discuss the technical details in Chapter 2), it was now free to do so and he urged them to rebalance the portfolio by selling off long leases – or at any rate not granting any more – and buying equities.

What Richardson would surely have liked to do, had he had the information, was look at the components of the portfolio by value rather than by net income. From this perspective the picture is even worse. Gilts and equities were traded frequently and their value was typically based on the stream of payments one expected from them. Therefore net income was a reasonable

---

147 SJC ADM III.A.14 (21 Oct. 1959).

proxy for value. The same was true of rack rents, although this did not account for the possibility that rack-rented farmland might become available for development at some stage, handing the owner a windfall. But the net income from the long leases – 14 per cent of the College's net income – definitely understated their value. Historic inflation meant that in some cases the annual ground rent on a property now amounted to just 1.25 per cent of the rack rent it would command.[148] The value was therefore mainly in the reversion of the property to the College at the end of the lease, so net income was a very poor proxy. Thus the College's endowment was even more concentrated in North Oxford than those figures suggest. And with no valuations of property carried out, it seems as if everyone until Richardson had simply missed this crucial fact.

The understated minutes from the finance committee and then Governing Body don't give much of an indication of the concern that Richardson's memo might have aroused. But their actions do. While still open to redeveloping Walton Manor, the Fellows resolved to begin divesting themselves of other property immediately. A report on the estate was commissioned to establish what this would look like in practice. Different areas of the estate were categorised: some for preservation; some for accommodation for College Fellows and servants; some for sale. The strategy was to sell off the lowest-quality parts, using some of the cash realised to redevelop the rest and some to shift the endowment into a more diverse mix of financial assets. After decades of sloth, the College was showing haste. But then the complaints started coming in.

---

148 SJC ADM III.C.1 (1953). Garrard writes, 'For example, a house let on a 99 years' Lease at a Ground Rent of £2.10s. might well command a Rack Rent of £200 a year' (p. 53).

This is the Record of John

Although the College's plans would have led to higher-density housing in parts of North Oxford, Lord Harcourt wanted more. From his perspective, it was a piece of incredible luck that an Oxford college owned so much of the building land in the city, and this was not an advantage to squander. The difficulty was in persuading a college which had just become aware of its financial vulnerability that engaging in such large-scale redevelopment was a sensible idea. Still, he did his best. Experts were brought in: a chartered surveyor

> said that in his opinion the College ought not to carry out the recommendations in the Joint Report (to sell outlying parts of the Estate) but should retain everything because, whereas there were any number of people only too anxious to carry out development and put up the money for such projects, there was a critical shortage of land and this priceless commodity should be held at all costs.[149]

Despite the idea of leasehold reform being in the air by this point, the surveyor felt that the prospect of leasehold enfranchisement – the idea that lessees should have the right to buy their properties from the lessor, possibly at a substantial discount – was not imminent. Norman Wates, a developer-builder, was similarly bullish: the College was, he said, 'sitting on a gold mine' – only unfortunately it was not one that could immediately be exploited, as the College would have to wait ten to twenty years for enough leases to fall in to make development practical.[150]

Only an advisor from Cluttons, the College's property

---

[149] SJC ADM III.B.106.
[150] Ibid.

advisors, sounded a cautious note. He argued that parts of the estate in the west were in such poor condition that only the council would have the resources (and, implicitly, the will) to redevelop them; as for the other areas, 'the political angle must be borne in mind. There is always a possibility that when a Labour Government is returned to power some sort of leasehold enfranchisement will be introduced to enable ground lessees who occupy their leasehold premises to buy the freehold reversion.'[151] No one seems to have made the fundamental point that, if the College was certain to get a large windfall *later*, it effectively had a large windfall *now*, as this future prosperity should be reflected in the potential sale price of the leasehold reversions. Unless the College added some particular value in playing a role in the development of North Oxford – and it is hard to see how it could, compared to a professional development company – it should be able to extract all the gold from its 'mine' simply by selling a parcel of land reversions to an interested third party.

The pressure worked. Richardson recanted his previous opinions in another note in 1962:

> My original recommendation to sell part of the North Oxford Estate was grounded on the desirability of spreading our risks. This general financial argument still holds ... Where I erred, however, was in taking too narrowly financial a standpoint. I had not appreciated fully the importance of unitary ownership for orderly development. I knew that particular areas should be kept intact but did not think in terms of developing North Oxford as a whole. Thus I believe now that the argument for diversifying the

---

151 SJC ADM III.B.106.

sources of our income may well be over-ridden, on social grounds, by the need not to fragment ownership.[152]

The note has a show-trial quality to it: much shorter and less data-driven than the one three years before, there is no sign of the careful economist attempting to quantify the trade-off inherent in considering the 'social grounds'. This is particularly notable given the confidence of his critics: the surveyor had said that 'If the properties are sold as suggested, I am quite certain that in a few years' time it will be shown <u>that they were greatly undersold</u>.'[153] But why would a chartered surveyor – however expert he might be in his field – have greater insight into designing a property portfolio than an economist?

As bursar, Garrard seems to have dutifully represented whatever the current College line was – after Governing Body voted to divest, he supported the plan and emphasised the political risks of not following it, writing: 'It seems a heavy burden to carry together with the increasing risk of political interference, and we may, in the end, have to make a decision on the financial sacrifice justifiable for the College to make in an attempt to preserve north Oxford in one ownership.'[154] But there is little doubt that he would have liked the College to remain patrician landlord to North Oxford. He was a dedicated servant of the College, keen on collecting rents in person, supervising the repair and decoration of houses on the estate, and generally running the show.

This could reach extremes. The 1950s involved running battles with tenants of farms over access to land and rights of way:

---

152 SJC MUN V.C.66.
153 SJC ADM II.C.3 (4 Dec. 1960, p. 8).
154 SJC ADM II.C.3 (20 Nov. 1961, p. 4).

> Our refusal to accept suggested rights-of-way over Upper Farm was contested by the Vicar with his militant spinsters and their four-legged friends ... when the Inspector commented on one person's evidence: 'Because you got away with going along this path doesn't necessarily mean you had a right to', there was really no doubt about the issue and the opposition there and then gave up.[155]

Doubtless the College's investments were protected by this and similar actions – just as the College prospered by Garrard's support of its pioneering farm and prize-winning pigs (the annual Bursar's Report was typically led by an update on their success in competitions). But while these actions may have been beneficial in themselves, they raise the question of prioritisation: what was the College's strategic vision for its endowment? This is what Richardson had been trying to achieve; it was (in a very different sense) something Lord Harcourt had done. Sadly, it was not what the rest of the Fellowship seems to have been focused on. The College ended up agreeing to wait. They would redevelop North Oxford when the leases fell in, and they would buy in those they could now – but there was no rush. They were sitting on a gold mine, after all. Everything was going to go on much as it always had.

Crisis

'There has been a reduction of the endowment, as the Bursar has advised us that owing to the effects of the white paper on leasehold reform, the value of urban sites let on long leases has

---

155 SJC ADM III.C.2 (1956, p. 35).

fallen by some £2,450,000.'[156] The Auditor's Report for 1965 does not dwell on this staggering loss, and moves on to its usual discussion of income statements and cost accounting. But they were almost irrelevant compared to the magnitude of the hit the College had taken.

The cause was, of course, the new Labour government's proposal to enfranchise leaseholders. As we have seen, the College had been warned about this: they had just not taken the risk seriously enough, lulled to sleep by 'experts' such as the chartered surveyor. Perhaps they simply found the thought too radical to take seriously – although other institutions in similar positions, such as Eton, were not so careless and had been taking capital out of their at-risk assets.[157] I discuss this issue in greater depth in Chapter 5: here it suffices to say that the College's loss was probably the result of poor judgement rather than bad luck.

The proposed legislation (it would only be enacted in 1967, after the government won a second election) was based on a simple principle, according to its proponents: that a lessee on a long lease (one of more than twenty-one years), morally – though not legally – 'owned' the property they lived in. The lessor, on the other hand, merely owned the land the property was built on. In effect this was an enormous giveaway to leaseholders with houses valued below the legislative limit, which included many in North Oxford. It meant that the reversions the College had been anticipating were not going to happen – or at least not for the buildings, which under the legislation represented most of the value. The College had started valuing its property portfolio in 1961, so we know that the £2.45m writedown represented about 90 per cent of the value of its long leases, 41 per cent of

---

156 SJC ADM III.C.32.
157 EC COLL/CHAL/1/1/7 p. 2.

its total property portfolio, and 34 per cent of its total investment assets. Adjusted for inflation, this is about £48m at the time of publication.¹⁵⁸ As a share of the College's wealth at time of publication – a more relevant measure – it represents about £253m.¹⁵⁹ And that does not account for the additional spending in the intervening decades which the enlarged endowment would have enabled.¹⁶⁰

I describe the legislation's tortured passage in more detail in Chapter 3. What is most remarkable is that St John's barely responded to the threat, not even joining other (less affected) landlords to lobby against the change or secure an exemption. Garrard did come up with a scheme to protect the College's ability to redevelop Walton Manor – and by extension protect the value of the houses there – by selling them to a housing association which the College set up and controlled, and which would be exempt from the enfranchisement law. All that happened was that the government got wind of the plans and changed the legislation so that housing associations were also covered by it, nullifying the College's attempt at legal evasion.¹⁶¹

Nonetheless, the change was not all bad. St John's now had to

---

158 This calculation is a conservative one, based on the real (i.e., inflation-adjusted) value of £2.45m in 1964. In practice, the College would have wanted an above-inflation return on its investments. Leaving them in long leases would have provided a low return, which would make this figure more realistic; on the other hand the College was hoping for improved investment returns and in practice its investments performed very well from 1980, meaning that it is probably a significant underestimate. See the Epilogue for more details.

159 Online Data, Financial Data, Endowment 2021.

160 If growth had been constant (it was not), there had been no donations (there were some) and the College, with perfect foresight of how its investments would prosper, had wished to spend 5 per cent of its endowment per year (it did not), then accounting for spending increases this figure to slightly over £3.3bn.

161 NA HLG 29/734.

divest from much of its North Oxford property, and it chose to divest even houses not covered by the legislation, winning praise in Parliament.[162] Since long leases were not an ideal asset class for the College to be invested in, this was an improvement. Peter Day, a chemistry Fellow, described the impact of the legislation:

> since many of the rents were controlled by legislation while repairs remained the responsibility of the ground landlord, it is fair to say that the overall yield from this part of the endowment was probably negative. The Finance Committee (quite properly the senior Governing Body subcommittee) must have been aware of the problem but, at least as far as I could see, never showed much inclination to do anything about it. In truth, in its torpor, the College was perfectly content with things the way they were, and apparently always had been … That this agreeable inanition came to an end – and the College set out on a new pathway towards the shape and stature we see today – was in fact the result of outside intervention [leasehold reform], unplanned and unlooked for.[163]

Day's is too rosy a view: as we have seen, the College had already considered divesting from long leases and was planning to redevelop North Oxford, which would have involved more detailed financial planning than they had engaged in over the last few decades. (Day may have been unaware of this: he joined the College as a Junior Research Fellow in 1964 and became an Official Fellow – sitting on Governing Body – two years later, so he was not around during the conversations in the early 1960s.)

---

162 *Hansard*. HC Deb. Vol. 784 Col. 755. (22 May 1969).
163 Day (2012) p. 80.

This would certainly have been a better result than taking the £2.45m hit. Nonetheless, his intuition that residential property was not an ideal sector to be in was correct. Government intervention throughout the twentieth century had squeezed most private landlords out of the sector, partially because the returns available were so low owing to rent control and other interventions. Returns to residential property were trending downwards from the 1960s, so even if the College had rack-rented many of the reverting properties it would not necessarily have been a good business for it to be in.[164] Furthermore, the sudden, and crucially uncontrolled, flow of money from enfranchisements ignited a debate in the College about how it should face the future.

It was a debate Governing Body was unused to – perhaps not since the days of Sidney Ball had the possibility of change been thrust upon them so directly. Although the Fellowship was fairly high powered by this point, its traditions harked back to an earlier era. Custodian of these was the Law Fellow, Edwin Slade. A classicist at St John's as a student, he had taken a good First and, everyone agreed, should become a Fellow. But there was no vacancy in Classics, so he was instead appointed as a Fellow in Law in 1929, and given the summer to gen up on the discipline. This is where things began to go wrong. Slade was clearly bright, and learned enough law to be called to the Bar. But it was not a good fit for him. The College considered making him a philosophy don, but stepped back when they realised it wouldn't improve matters – indeed, he was eventually

---

[164] Chambers, Spaenjers and Steiner (2021) p. 3591. Note that this paper is based on data from four Oxbridge Colleges but not St John's, Oxford; it also does not account for cases where the owner gets development rights (e.g., turning a farm into a housing estate) or long leases.

judged so unsuitable that jurisprudence was taught by the philosopher John Mabbott instead.[165] The only thing he appears to have published was a new edition of *Thomas & Bellot's Leading Cases in Constitutional Law*. His teaching was no better: Day recalled that 'He did not exert himself greatly, as the College's record in Law Finals testified.'[166] Or perhaps he just didn't have time – for Slade, the afternoons were for sport, especially cricket and tennis. By the end of his time at the College he was still insisting that his arcane post-prandial procedures be followed, and doing no significant academic work.[167]

What were these arcane procedures? After dining, the Fellows would retire to take second dessert (or 'Common Room'): a selection of fruits, lubricated with dessert wines. The fruits themselves were arranged in different bowls and positioned (and eaten) in order of precedence: 'major' fruits first (those indigenous to Britain) and 'minor' (those not privileged with a Britannic origin) subsequently.[168] The whole scheme was thrown into chaos when new information on the gooseberry came to light – the now humble fruit was promptly demoted. As one young observer said, you would think the whole thing was a pantomime, but Slade was completely serious.[169] The contrast between a body of increasingly academically distinguished men and the excessive formality imposed by one of the least notable – but nonetheless most senior – of their number is a microcosm of the broader institutional situation. In their field, Fellows could be exceptional; when it came to collective action,

---

165 Simpson (2021) p. 64.
166 Day (2012) p. 70.
167 Multiple private conversations.
168 Thomas in Harrison (1994) p. 198.
169 Private conversation.

tradition was the order of the day. But now events were forcing them to make decisions.

There were two grand projects, which swiftly became interrelated. First, the College decided to double down on the success of the Beehive by building a new quadrangle north-east of North Quad, which would allow them to house all their undergraduates, as well as an expanded graduate population. The project would be expensive and architecturally adventurous, and there was much debate about what form it should take and what facilities it should grace the College with. Second, President Mabbott announced his intention to retire. Like his predecessor Costin, Mabbott had been an undergraduate at the College and a Fellow since the early 1920s. Who was to replace him, and lead the expansion project?

The Fellowship began to rustle up candidates.[170] Six Fellows were thought to deserve a shot at the top job, and sixteen external men were also suggested. The Vice-President set up a two-track winnowing process, holding a series of semi-formal votes to cut both groups down to a more manageable number. Once only seven externals remained, two Fellows per candidate were assigned to construct dossiers on their man, so the others could judge whether they were the right sort. Further voting followed, and eventually a clear victor emerged: Richard Southern, a medievalist and the Chichele Professor of Modern History at All Souls. (Oxford, liking to keep things in perspective, considers 'modern' history to have begun in 476 with the fall of the Western Roman Empire.) Next came the delicate question of inviting him to take up the position – for, as was typical at the time, none of the external candidates had been told they were

---

170 The description that follows is based on SJC MUN LIII.A.138, 140, the latter of which is sealed.

candidates, and it was not considered at all certain that he would sacrifice his research for administration. Indeed, he had already turned down what might be regarded as the more glittering prize of the Mastership of Balliol. But after some deliberation Southern did accept the offer, exhorting the Fellows, 'Please don't think that my delay in coming to this point has been due to any lack of warmth on my part. The generosity of the College's proposal has been constantly in my mind ... But I knew you would prefer a considered judgment to a merely instinctual response.'[171]

What made Southern – a brilliant historian at the height of his powers, who probably could have stayed on at All Souls as Warden had he wanted a more relaxed managerial role – decide to take the job? Hugh Trevor-Roper, the Regius Professor of Modern History, famously struggled to understand how 'Master Southern ha[d] judged it elevation to go from that chair to preside over St John's coll., a dull place north of Balliol but monstrous rich.'[172] One factor seems to have been the opportunities for engaging with students and developing Oxford educationally – All Souls was the only college with no students (other than the odd Prize Fellow) and thus no teaching.

The election also reveals a great deal about the Fellowship's priorities. The past two presidents had both been the most senior Fellows in the College – the most senior this time round was Slade, whom no one nominated, but other senior internal candidates were put forward. Things had changed, however, and there was a definite appetite among the Fellowship for an external candidate. Harold Thompson, the brilliant chemist who was second in seniority, suggested no fewer than four academically

---

171 SJC MUN LIII.A.138 (16 July 1968).
172 Trevor-Roper (1970) p. 32.

distinguished externals for the job. Keith Thomas chose a more targeted approach. He seems to have identified Southern, whom he had known at All Souls, early on as a potential president, and he backed his man to the hilt: the numerous glowing references in his file, solicited by Thomas or written by him following conversations with colleagues, extol the medievalist as intellectually brilliant, managerially competent, enthusiastic about expansion, and above all 'an outstandingly good man'. This is not to say that the other files were empty: the Fellows seem to have taken their responsibilities seriously, gathering evidence of both academic and managerial distinction, and garnering several replies suggesting that this or that candidate, while a wonderful person, might not be up to the job for various reasons. When the election took place it showed that these reports had been taken into account, with voting behaviour changing accordingly. But the sheer mass of supporting documentation gathered by Thomas meant the Fellows could literally feel the gravity of the man.

Change also came to the Bursary. After eighteen long years of service, Garrard retired and Harry Kidd – a former undergraduate at St John's, now escaping from his position as school secretary at the London School of Economics after student protests roiled the small campus and (arguably indirectly) resulted in the death of a porter – was appointed in his place.[173] An expert in charities law but not investment, he set about farming out the College's advisory duties to external contractors.[174] Anachronisms such as

---

173 Kidd describes the events in *The Troubles at L.S.E., 1966–1967* (1969). St John's only features obliquely: 'The staff were painfully divided, counting the cost and licking their wounds. For my part, I was ceasing to be a close observer of events at the School, with my mind turning to a new range of problems that were waiting for me elsewhere' (p. 119).
174 SJC ADM III.A.12 (2 Oct. 1967).

the housing association were unwound.[175] There were limits to this rationalisation – St John's still lacked a chartered accountant – and the choice of investment manager was not especially successful, with returns in the difficult economic climate of the 1970s being rather lacklustre. Unimpressed, some Fellows took action. In 1974 John Kay, a new Fellow in Economics hired in 1970, helped establish an investment sub-committee and gradually took on more and more responsibility, eventually becoming Investment Officer and delivering the over-performance that is the basis of the College's wealth today.[176] (But that is a story for the Epilogue.) Equally important was the decision to hire John Montgomery as the College accountant: remarkably he seems to have been the first chartered accountant to be employed in that capacity by the University or any of its colleges! Through rigorous cost control alone he saved the College millions when its Garden Quadrangle was built in the 1990s.[177]

The Fellowship were probably more receptive to the need for such financial strictures, having experienced the chaos involved in building the Sir Thomas White building which bounded the new quadrangle. Inflation, and the usual cost overruns, meant that the budget had threatened to spiral completely out of control. The architect, Philip Dowson, had also designed University College's North Oxford annexe (known as Stavertonia) shortly before, and its construction had been beset by similar problems. He recalled that, unlike at University College, Southern had asked him upfront for advice – 'He admitted that he had been to school, to university and then to All Souls, and he did not know much about the wicked world' – and took it,

---

[175] SJC ADM III.A.12 (22 Nov. 1967).
[176] SJC ADM III.A.24 (19 June 1974).
[177] Private correspondence.

distributing additional money upfront to avoid a costly reorganisation of contractors in the long term.[178] As a result, the whole project went off much more smoothly – or so Dowson's story goes, although other academics on the committee remember the negotiations somewhat differently. In any case, the building eventually opened in 1975, having cost about £1.5m (only slightly exceeding the budget of £1.24m) and enabled the College to provide all undergraduate students with accommodation throughout their degrees.[179] Just like the Beehive, it won multiple awards, and an appreciation of its striking design can temporarily distract the viewer from remembering how ugly it really is. (Sadly the opportunity to honour the President and confuse guests by naming the quadrangle Southern Quad was not taken.)

The College's endowment performance (including income generated and spent by the College) was less dramatic. As Figure 1.4 shows, once we adjust the College's endowment to account for the high inflation in the 1970s, it barely increases from 1961 to 1980 (although it does recover from the dip in 1965 when the value of the long leaseholds are written down). Maintaining a constant endowment in real terms is not necessarily a sign of failure: the College may have been drawing heavily on it to fund its activities. Examining the rates of return, however, shows that its performance varied. From 1965 (when we begin to have reasonable data) the College's investments returned, on average, 0.8 per cent below inflation annually; simply holding the FTSE100 index would have returned about 3.9 per cent, suggesting that efforts to pick stocks were very unsuccessful. On the other hand, real property returned 7.1 per cent above inflation

---

178 Interview with Philip Dowson by Robin Darwall-Smith.
179 Tyack (2005) p. 65.

This is the Record of John

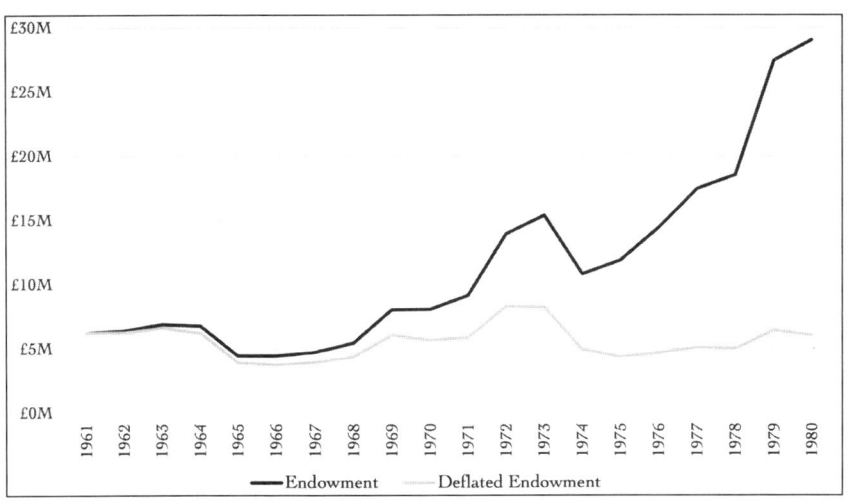

Figure 1.4: Endowment Performance

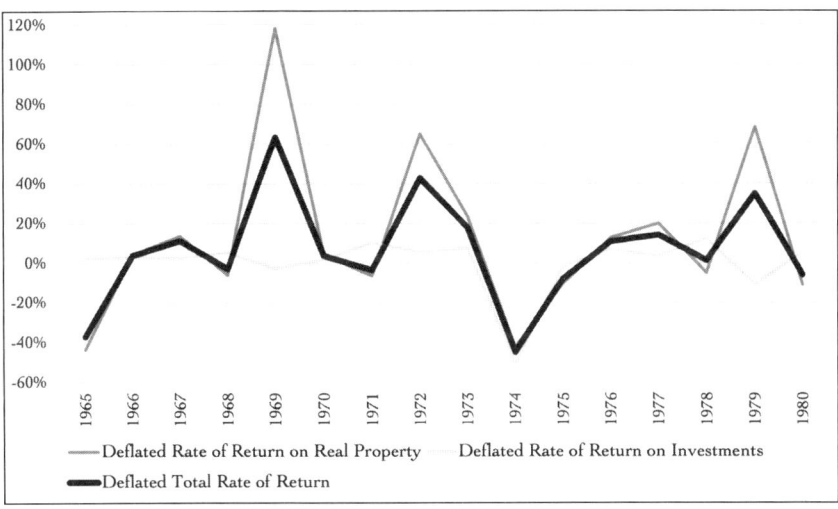

Figure 1.5: Relative Rates of Return

– but it became steadily less important over the period as the College sold it and used the funds to buy equities. Overall the College achieved a real return of 3.5 per cent: not awful but certainly not spectacular. Although investment performance was very poor, the damage to the value of the long leaseholds was the main culprit: but for that, the College's return would have been almost twice as high.

There is a widespread belief that Southern was responsible for the transformation of the College academically. To some extent this is clearly true: as well as shepherding the Sir Thomas White Building to completion he pushed for an expansion of the number of Tutorial Fellows to support the students, and the SCR duly exploded in size. As President he was active in calling for high academic standards: John Carey, the English Fellow, remembered him as 'Lean, witty and an intellectual to his fingertips ... something of the medieval abbot hung about him, and it was jokingly said that when the St John's examination results were worse than expected he would call the College together for prayer and fasting.'[180] But the change was not immediate, as Figure 1.6 with the College's Norrington Table performance shows, and the College's academic dominance was mainly enjoyed by his successor. (The Norrington Table ranked colleges based on how well their undergraduates did in the final exams compared to how well they theoretically could have done.)[181]

---

180 Carey (2015) p. 241.
181 When these comparisons were first explicitly made in the 1950s, colleges were ranked by the proportion of first-class degrees received. This quickly turned into a weighted system where getting a First got you three points, a Second got two points, and a Third got one point. Each college's total score was then divided by their theoretical maximum, i.e., three times the number of undergraduates taking Final Honour Schools that year. In 1986 *The Times*, which published the tables, adopted the weighting system used by the Tompkins Table in Cambridge, where a First

This is the Record of John

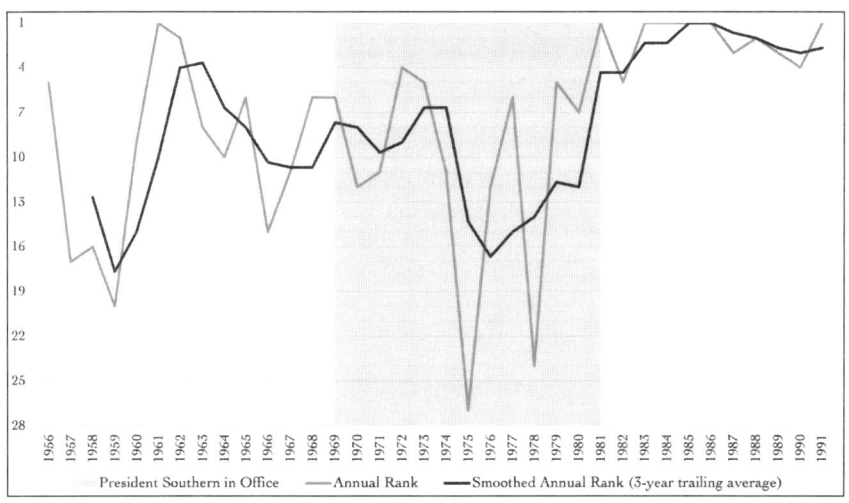

Figure 1.6: The College's Norrington Table Ranking

I address the question of exactly how much of a role Southern played in Chapter 4.

Even before the change had fully set in, however, observers noticed the difference. The *College Record* for 1973–4 notes with relief improved examination results, as 'befits a Laudian establishment'.[182] Perhaps it is no surprise that it was in the same year that the *Record* included the ghostly epilogue describing Laud pacing in his old library, flecking with light the ancient walls. Something of his spirit had indeed returned.

---

was worth five points, a 2:i three points; a 2.ii two points, and a Third one point. Applying either system does not change the results dramatically, and so I have used the more modern system throughout.

182 *College Record* (1974) p. 12.

2

ET IN ARCADIA EGO

The College's Portfolio Problem

> A Good Business Man ... is one whose mind has not been warped and narrowed by merely intellectual interests, and who, at the same time, has not those odious pushing qualities which are unhappily required for making a figure in business anywhere else ... While you are engaged in Boring it does not matter much what you talk about; but, if possible, you should discourse upon the proper way of doing something which you are notorious for doing badly yourself. Thus ... if you are a good business man, you should discuss the principles of finance and so on.
>
> F. M. Cornford, *Microcosmographica Academica*, 1908

Today, the College's endowment is invested in a variety of different asset classes: just over half is in financial assets and the rest is in property. The lion's share of financial assets – just over 90 per cent – are equities, from a variety of countries (but mainly developed ones). Another 8 per cent or so is in funds; the difference is made up by fixed-income stocks. Even this minuscule proportion, however, overstates their role in the College's portfolio, as two loans (one secured against the Kendrew

Quadrangle) totalling £75m have been taken out: one in 2010 to take advantage of the low interest rates the College had access to and invest in equities; the other in 2016, taking advantage of the demand for debt from credible borrowers with a maturity of over thirty years, which was used to buy dollars to hedge against the possibility of Brexit. The portfolio is also distinctive in having a relatively small exposure to hedge funds, private equity, and other alternative assets – although the substantial wine cellars are not included. Property is held across the world – for example, St John's owns an apartment block in Berlin and another in Seattle. Closer to home, it continues the tradition of Oxonian property development through the unimaginatively named Oxford North, an 'innovation district' near Wolvercote. This portfolio is the product of considerable thought and expertise on the part of various financial professionals; it draws on standard financial theory (which explains its considerable diversity) but, like other Oxbridge college portfolios, also expresses strong views about the current state of financial markets (that fixed income is generally overvalued; that there are worthwhile land-development opportunities in Britain; and that the value added net of fees by many funds is questionable).[1]

As we saw in the previous chapter, it has not always been like this. George Richardson raised the alarm over how concentrated the endowment was, and how little exposure it had to equities, in 1959; if St John's had not been forced to divest itself of much of its property after 1967 this state of affairs might have persisted for even longer than it did. Why has the College's portfolio ever looked different to the way it does now?

---

[1] For an analysis of Oxbridge college portfolios relative to American university endowments see Dimson and Acharya (2007). Their analysis is based on interviews conducted in 2002–3.

Et in Arcadia Ego

What Could the College Do?

As ecclesiastical and charitable foundations, Oxbridge colleges have always been restricted in how they manage their financial affairs – particularly land that was given to them at their endowment. They only gained a general power to sell such land in 1856, and if they did the money was held by the Board (later Ministry) of Agriculture until it was reinvested in different land (or sometimes in very safe government securities).[2] In 1898 the law was changed to allow investment in other fixed-income securities, and (if the college passed a statute explicitly authorising this) other forms too. In 1961, trustees were allowed to invest half their funds in stocks and shares (and three-quarters in 1966); and in 1964 control passed from the Ministry to the colleges.

Assets held at the Ministry of Agriculture were further divided into 'free capital' and sinking funds. The idea of a sinking fund was that, if you sold an asset which would have appreciated in value over time (like a house on a long lease which would eventually revert to the college), you might be accessing money now at the expense of money in the future. To avoid this, the value of the property at a given point in the future was estimated, along with any income it would have produced up to that point; the Ministry then assumed a suitable rate of interest and worked out the annual payments the college needed to make to build up a fund such that, on the given date, the same value had accrued. These funds would be invested in fixed-income securities. The idea was fairly sound – if you had an asset yielding 5 per cent and you could buy one yielding 8 per cent for the same price, then you could complete the transaction, pay 5 per cent of the yield into the sinking fund, and enjoy the other 3 per cent. On the other hand, if the alternative asset offered a yield of only 4 per

---

[2] Dunbabin (1975) p. 631; Neild (2008) pp. 87–8.

cent then you would not find the deal attractive. But a simpler way of looking at the situation is just to say that the first example is a good deal, and the second one a bad deal, and you would hope bursars could tell the difference without the apparatus of a sinking fund. Sinking funds also created other issues: if you held on to the house you'd get income from it each year, whereas if you sold it that income would become part of the sinking fund value you would need to build up, potentially leaving you worse off in the short term even if selling the house made sense. Furthermore, the sinking fund consisted of fixed-income securities which may not have been the most appropriate investment assets for a college.

Even free capital was not all that free: if a college wanted to embark on a building project, they would have to agree a 'loan' with the Ministry of Agriculture, whereby they would 'lend' *themselves* money from their free capital and agree to pay it back over time. Free capital was built up by investment performance and by sinking funds: once the set time period had passed the fund became free capital.

In contrast to endowed capital, colleges were always permitted to invest non-endowed capital in equities if they wished. The general opinion of the Oxbridge college bursars, however, seems to have been that equities were an inappropriate form of investment: as well as being too risky, they threatened to reduce the colleges' independence vis-à-vis the University because, as one bursar noted, if they did not hold land they would be seen as 'glorified hostels ... that ... ought to be put under the central management of some University Delegacy ... It may also be remarked, that confiscation of Stocks and Securities is a simpler matter than that of lands.'[3] Thus in practice investment

---
3 Quoted in Dunbabin (1994) p. 659.

Et in Arcadia Ego

in equities before the Second World War was almost unheard of.

King's College, Cambridge is the sole exception. It changed its statutes in 1927 to allow investment of some of its endowment in equities – but this was because John Maynard Keynes was its bursar and wanted to.[4] Although he offered advice to other Cambridge colleges none seem to have followed his bold move; for example Trinity College, Cambridge only changed its own statutes to allow such investment in 1946, and that seems to have been due to pressure from alumni who had careers in the City of London. Its bursar, while supporting the change, commented, 'I cannot say that I am at all looking forward to a large extension of my responsibilities and to having to learn a new technique.'[5] Some of the other colleges with larger endowments also began to invest at this stage, with All Souls buying some equities in 1945 and Christ Church in 1948.[6] Further loosening of control followed after 1949, when Corpus Christi College, Cambridge wrote a new investment statute giving its bursar more power than trusts normally had, and this became a model for other colleges.[7] It therefore seems likely that it was Keynes's force of personality, and undoubted expertise, that explains King's College's pioneering move.

What about other investors? The wealthy formed the majority of stock-market participants in Britain in the nineteenth century. David Cannadine has described how the aristocracy sold their lands (and other assets) from the late nineteenth century onwards, and after debts were paid off much of the proceeds

---

4 Neild (2008) p. 122; King's College, Cambridge (1927) Statute D.IV and Ordinance D.4.7.
5 Neild (2008) p. 122.
6 Dunbabin (1994) p. 671.
7 Rogers (2011) p. 686.

went into equities.⁸ He notes that they tended to do very well from the trade, although the explanation that equities were 'a safer investment, and obtain[ed] a greater return' is not wholly convincing, implying as it does that the people who (effectively) traded equities for the assets the aristocrats were offloading were fools. It seems likely that regulation and an ingrained conservatism when it came to financial affairs harmed institutions and made these trades appear more attractive than they were.⁹ Neither do the middle classes seem to have played a significant role in equity investment until the Second World War, although the public at the time thought that they did.¹⁰ (There was also some participation on the margins: those without access to the stock exchange could trade what were effectively options on stock prices in 'bucket shops'.¹¹)

Shares could also be held indirectly, through pension or insurance funds, but these tended to be invested in fixed income and some property: as late as 1939, individuals owned 80 per cent of the shares on the London Stock Exchange.¹² What would be described as the 'cult of equity' was primarily a post-war phenomenon. Exceptions include the Imperial Tobacco pension fund, which had started adding equities in 1933 – although by 1947 these only accounted for 20 per cent of its portfolio. Other funds were more cautious: in 1945 just 10 per cent of pension fund assets were in equities.¹³

---

8   Cannadine (1990) pp. 121–35.
9   Ibid. p. 122.
10 For the lack of participation see Maltby et al. (2011) pp. 203–4; for the opinions at the time see Rutterford, Green, Maltby and Owens (2011) pp. 162–3; for change after the Second World War see Heinemann (2016) p. 262.
11 Heinemann (2016) p. 258.
12 Davies (2017) p. 39.
13 Avrahampour (2015) pp. 1–2.

The situation differed somewhat in the United States where university endowments, despite having similar trustee restrictions to their British equivalents, were moving into equities – cautiously in the 1920s, then more enthusiastically in the 1930s.[14] Intriguingly, R. B. McCallum, a historian with enough economic acumen (or at least confidence) to take on Keynes's *The Economic Consequences of the Peace*, wrote an article for the *Oxford Magazine* in 1933 where, in the aftermath of Britain's departure from the gold standard and the damage this did to fixed-income investments, he called on universities to be allowed to invest in equities.[15] He had spent a year at Princeton in 1922–3 and possibly had picked up on the new ideas there. In general, however, colleges – and the people and institutions they would have compared themselves with – were suspicious of, and inexperienced with, equities.

And even non-endowed capital might not be sufficiently free to invest as the college saw fit. It was typical for donations of capital to a college to be made for some particular purpose, and in these cases the assets would go into a trust, typically named for the donor and with instructions that the income was to be spent on specified objects. For example, the Lambe Trust was set up to fund the William Lambe Scholarship at St John's. Historically these trusts were managed discretely, but colleges began

---

14 Goetzmann, Griswold and Tseng (2010), Exhibits 1, 3, 5, 8; Chambers, Dimson and Kaffe (2020), Figure 1.
15 McCallum (1931); his critique of Keynes was published as *Public Opinion and the Last Peace* (1944). Indeed, the book 'about which I lost my temper at the time and kept it lost' annoyed him so much that it led him to inaugurate the Nuffield election studies, writing *The British General Election of 1945* (1947) with Alison Readman so that there would be no repeat of 'the short, slight and sketchy remarks about the 1918 election' Keynes had popularised. He expressed his aim more succinctly as 'Keynes and all that rot. We'll have no more of that.' (Quoted in Butler, 1998, p. 451.)

to combine them into a single 'Trusts Fund', which would be invested as a single portfolio and in which the individual trust funds had shares. Such funds were not subject to the control of the Ministry of Agriculture, but the trustees were bound by the law to invest in 'trustee securities': a list including gilts, corporation stocks, and mortgages but not equities.

And then there were idiosyncratic restrictions: for example, in 1958 the College considered buying shares in Shell for its free capital account but could not do the same for the Trusts Fund as the fund's statutes forbade investment in oil companies.[16] This was the origin of the oil investments that would, many decades later, lead to controversy for the investment sub-committee when protesters 'occupied' Front Quad, calling for divestment.[17] However, the Trusts Fund restriction was not for environmental reasons but because the statutes prohibited owning shares in companies whose 'main business [is] ... the ownership working or exploitation of minerals or other wasting assets'.[18] The idea seems to have been that an oil company was basically a collection of wells that would eventually be exhausted; recognising that Shell was better described as a company with a distinctive capability for getting oil out of the ground, the College judged it an appropriate investment.

Finally, St John's was an organisation busy spending and taking in money: charging fees for tuition and rent; running a kitchen; managing its own farm and Bagley Wood. It therefore needed some cash on hand, and conceivably might end up with too much cash on hand: this could be invested through the revenue account. On top of this, the College maintained an

---

16 SJC ADM III.A.14 (9 Dec. 1958).
17 SJC ADM III.C.25.
18 St John's College (1956) p. 77.

insurance fund (to lower the insurance payments it made) and pension funds (the fund for Fellows began in 1926 following a change in the statutes; one for College servants appears to have preceded it).[19] In practice the pension funds ended up being managed as part of the Trusts Fund.

The environment, therefore, was complex, and the legal situation often unclear. Keynes's experience at King's exemplifies this. When he got involved in the college's finances in 1919 he quickly persuaded them to set up a new 'discretionary' account, which unlike the 'restricted' account could invest in non-trustee securities. But even this step was considered potentially illegal (which, some claimed, is why Keynes consistently opposed King's hiring a Fellow in Law) and the justification seems to have been that the college's statutes, before being updated in 1927, were fairly loose.[20] Still, changing statutes required an Order in Council, suggesting that the move had received official sanction – but it was a pioneering move, and as late as 1947 the University of Oxford received an opinion of counsel stating that all college property should be treated as being held in trust and so only eligible for conversion into trustee securities.[21] For most colleges, it probably seemed that both the letter and the spirit of the law of investments was conservative.

---

19 SJC ADM III.B.6; SJC ADM III.D.1 (1918).
20 Moggridge (1992) pp. 351–2; King's College, Cambridge (1927) Statute D.IV and Ordinance D.4.7. They remained quite loose: '(7) The Bursar in charge of investments shall have power to invest surplus funds, and to change existing investments, subject to any restrictions which may be laid down by the Estates Committee.'
21 SJC ADM III.Various Subjects.206.

What Should the College Have Done?

As is often the case, academic theory lagged some way behind practice. Empirical evidence of the 'equity premium' – the stylised fact that, even accounting for their increased volatility, equities tend to reliably return more than other asset classes over the long run – began to appear in the 1920s.[22] Around the same time, discounted cashflow valuation, the modern way of valuing equities, began to be popularised.[23] In the 1950s Harry Markowitz's Modern Portfolio Theory gave investors tools to consider the trade-off between risk and reward in their portfolios.[24] Work was also beginning on strategies that were 'growth-optimal' in the long run.[25]

Nonetheless, many of the important insights were already relatively well known. Merchants have avoided committing all their resources to a single venture for millennia. Investors knew to put money into high-quality companies, with manageable debt burdens and reputable boards – thus avoiding the problem of moral hazard, where managers knew the business was worth less than others thought but would take their capital. And although inflation had not been a significant factor for much of the nineteenth century, the First World War and then Britain's departure from the gold standard had shown that it was a real risk for assets which paid out fixed nominal returns. Even if investors did not have the mathematical tools and computational power available today, thoughtful ones had access to much of the intuition the theory provided. (Markowitz himself

---

22 See Goetzmann, Griswold and Tseng (2010) pp. 119–20 for a summary.
23 For example Fisher (1930).
24 Markowitz (1952).
25 Christensen (2012); see Ford and Kay (2022) for the limitations of these approaches.

wrote that 'What was lacking prior to 1952 was an adequate theory of investment' but, as *The Merchant of Venice* showed, 'Clearly, Shakespeare not only knew about diversification but, at an intuitive level, understood covariance.'[26])

Given these tools, what should an institution like a college do? It is unrealistic to expect market-beating performance unless they have some special advantage, as King's did through Keynes's expertise. What is feasible is thinking carefully about overall investment aims and investing in a balance of different assets that will do as good a job as possible of meeting those aims in a range of conditions. It is important that an endowment generates enough income to keep its institution liquid (as St John's failed to do in the aftermath of the First World War). Since money has been given in trust for the future, it is important to maintain its real capital value, and to ensure it earns a decent return.

In practice these two aims butted up against each other. Maximising income generation was the rule for much of the twentieth century. Maximising total return (capital gains as well as income) is a more recent concept, and despite seeming to be the only sensible way to measure return it often rubs against our intuitions – possibly because such a policy may involve selling assets in order to access income. The two aims give different perspectives on investment projects: institutions can generally get more income now at the expense of capital growth, but this will do long-term harm if it is not accounted for.

A second factor to consider is risk. To some extent we expect a trade-off between risk and return: gilts return a specified stream of payments guaranteed by the government whereas a company share pays an uncertain dividend, so there is a premium for

---

26 Markowitz (1999) p. 5.

the certainty gilts provide. But risk is a much broader concept than whether or not a particular investment behaves as you hope it will. For a college, risk is best understood as the possibility that its (reasonable) investment aims are not met.[27] If the entire endowment is in rare wines which have become very valuable – but for which there is, annually, only very limited demand – then the college may not be able to generate sufficient endowment income and a risk will have been realised, even if – quite correctly – the endowment is judged to have performed very well. If gilts pay out exactly what they were expected to, but the value of that money has declined because inflation has driven the college's costs up more than it expected, then a risk will have been realised. And if much of the endowment is put into a specific sector of the economy and then those companies suffer from an unexpected downturn, destroying value, then a risk will have been realised.

A portfolio should reflect a balance between these two factors, as well as being influenced by specific factors about the institution. For St John's, this translates to a portfolio that will see a reasonable level of growth and is unlikely to be too adversely affected by plausible market conditions. So concerns about inflation are very important – the College employs a lot of staff and wage inflation is historically higher than general price inflation – whereas liquidity concerns may not be so relevant (the College plans to exist for ever, and so if an investment gives a good return but can't be realised any time soon, then, as long as it's not too large a fraction of the portfolio, that's fine).[28]

---

27 Here I am following the definition of risk expounded in Kay and King (2020) pp. 122–4, 305–10, 332, 421.
28 One reason that wage inflation tends to rise faster than price inflation is that productivity (hopefully) grows over time and this is reflected in wages. From that

This analysis suggests a portfolio weighted towards assets with exposure to the real economy – equities and real estate where income is regularly updated, perhaps alongside some alternative assets such as wine, forests, etc. – but diversified within those categories as much as is feasible.

What Did the College Actually Do?

Compared to other contemporary institutions, St John's did not stand out. In 1952 it altered its statutes to allow for limited equity investment by its Trusts Fund, and we see it using the new powers immediately as it ends the year with £11,131 invested.[29] This represented just under 3 per cent of the College's invested funds, which does not include its substantial investments in real property. But it only changed its statutes to allow investment of its free capital in equities in 1956.[30] By 1959, when Richardson was worrying about the College's excessive exposure to property, ordinary shares represented just under 60 per cent of the value of invested funds in its free capital and Trusts Fund. It seems that deciding whether or not to invest in equities had been the bottleneck: once that decision was reached the College implemented it rapidly. However, Figures 2.1 and 2.2 show that even by 1961 (when property valuations were first completed) the financial investments were dwarfed by the

---

perspective, wage inflation is no more serious than price inflation, as the College would still get the same real product of labour. But productivity growth does not tend to be equal across sectors of the economy, and it seems unlikely that academic productivity has increased as much as that of other workers.

29 SJC MUN LXXX.33; SJC ADM III.C.19. The relevant figure is for Commercial and Industrial Securities not redeemable by a fixed date.
30 SJC MUN LXXX.37.

Intellectual Capital

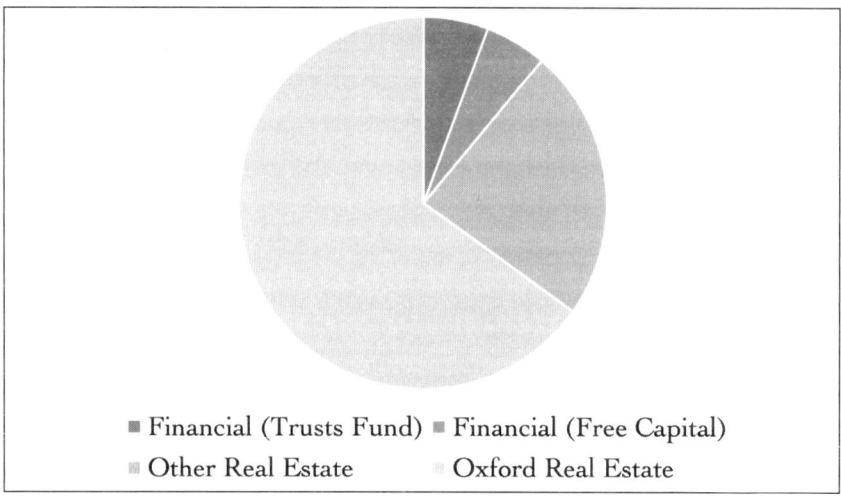

Figure 2.1: St John's College's Portfolio 1961

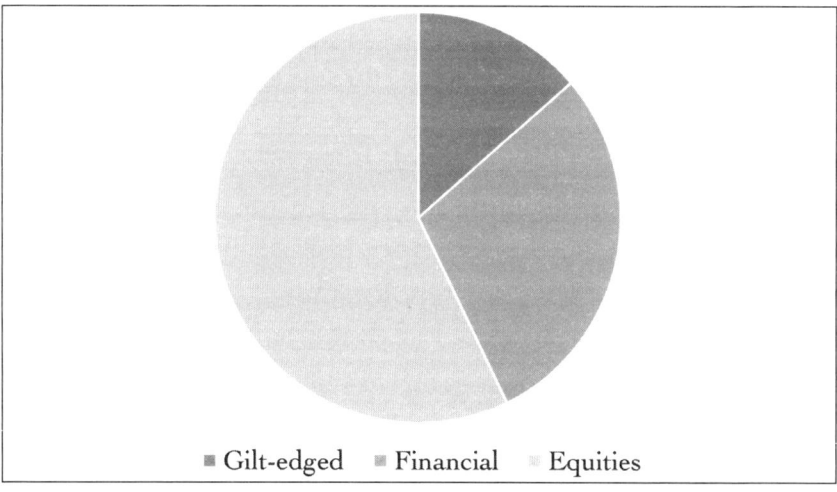

Figure 2.2: Free Capital at the Ministry of Agriculture 1961

role of property.[31] The overwhelming majority of the College's endowment income was coming from real estate, despite long leases having performed relatively badly.

As Figure 2.1 shows, the College's net income had historically been overwhelmingly dependent on land.[32] But the proportions changed: houses on long leases went from providing almost half of the income to providing less than 20 per cent, reflecting the damage caused by inflation. Houses on rack rents, on the other hand, became a much larger source of income as the rents could be adjusted – albeit with limits due to rent restrictions – to reflect inflation. And income from financial assets remained low until the mid-1950s, when the College's investments in equities began to increase it – in the 1960s equities typically yielded much more than bonds. In terms of both wealth and income, the College remained highly exposed to a single type of property, much of which was in a single location.

As described in the previous chapter, the Fellows were then warned about this exposure and prevaricated, with disastrous consequences. One happy result, however, was that the College finally undertook a valuation of its property portfolio in 1961 (a process subsequently repeated, if erratically). Figure 2.4 shows the effect of leasehold reform on the endowment (in 1965, as the College wrote down the value of its long leases upon the publication of the White Paper on enfranchisement) and we can see how financial investments became relatively more important for the College (and continued to be up to 1980), while still being subordinate to real property.

---

31 SJC ADM III.C.26.
32 SJC ADM III.A.14.

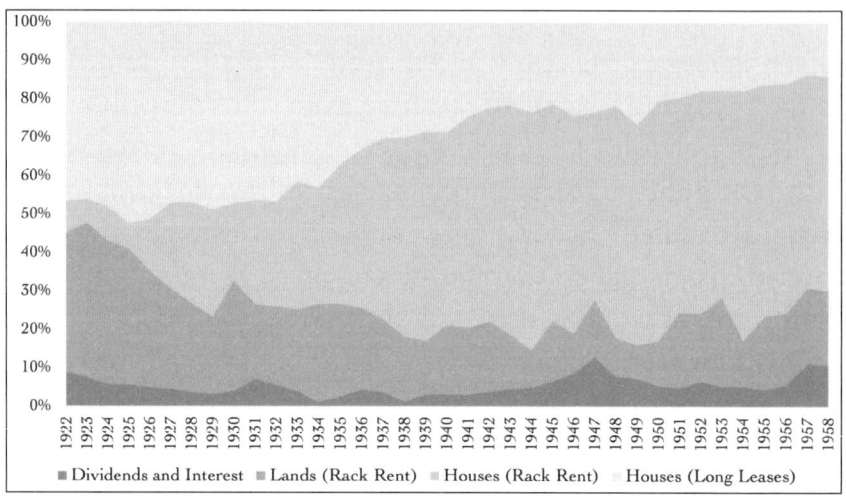

Figure 2.3: Net Income by Asset Class

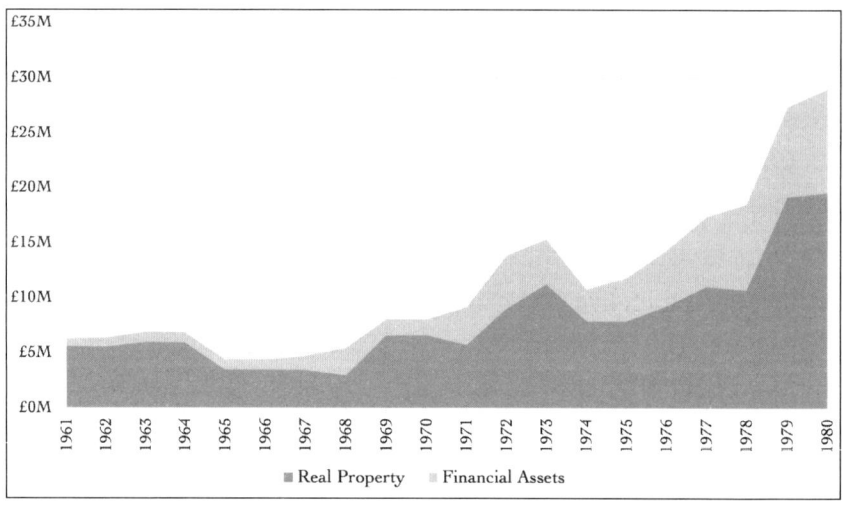

Figure 2.4: Endowment Value by Asset Type

The Portfolio Problem

Given the legal restrictions and the state of financial knowledge in the 1950s and 60s, there are three major questions about the College's portfolio. First, why was it so exposed to North Oxford – and the political risk surrounding housing – rather than being more diversified? Second, why were its investments so tilted towards assets generating (relatively) fixed nominal income? And third, how did it understand its North Oxford Estate: as an investment; as a paternalistic project; or as something else?

As we saw in the previous chapter, exposure to North Oxford was for the most part historically determined, with long leases being a sensible way to manage development risk while retaining control of the estate. The College's exposure was a consequence of the success of this development, meaning that the portfolio became unbalanced simply as a result of following the status quo. And there were reasons for inertia. Unlike most trustee securities, which typically had deep, liquid markets, every building was idiosyncratic. Investors might be expected to have a view on how much they were willing to pay for a particular gilt or share in a company, but to decide how much to spend on buying the long lease on a house in North Oxford they would need to undertake expensive due diligence on the property and relevant covenants. The transaction costs associated with divesting from the estate were therefore significantly higher than with other assets, and the pool of potential buyers was smaller, decreasing the chance that the College would find a buyer offering a reasonable amount.

On top of this, the estate had more value as an integrated whole than as a bundle of buildings and land. As a single landowner St John's could, and did, invest in public goods that would augment the value of all the properties: planting trees; funding churches and other charitable bodies; and enforcing the covenants that kept the residents from annoying one another (too much). Many of the opportunities to put these public goods in place arose when the estate was first planned and built, and it is important to note that the College's ability to produce this additional value declined over time as the city council's role in managing the estate grew. By 1885 the local board of health had taken over the roads and the College was paying it to build new ones as and when needed, with residents paying rates to the city for their upkeep.[33] Nonetheless, operating an estate as an integrated whole remains a business proposition today, and some estates have been able to unlock significant value through this approach. There was genuine financial value, therefore, in keeping the North Oxford Estate intact.

Keeping the estate meant that the College was heavily invested, not just in North Oxford, but in residential property. Unfortunately, this was not an ideal asset class for an institution to hold, because, quite apart from the eventual reforms to leaseholds, the twentieth century had seen a stream of legislation restricting the ability of landlords to determine rents. These restrictions were intended to be temporary – the first, in 1915, were designed to stop price gouging during the First World War – but were somehow never fully repealed. The residential rental sector was progressively squeezed until by 1975 it represented just 16 per cent of the market, down from 90 per cent before the First World War.[34] It also reduced the return landlords could achieve: in this period residential property, on average, saw real annual gross income 'growth' of minus 1 per cent![35] Furthermore, large amounts had to be spent on maintaining such

---

33 SJC MUN V.B.138.i (7 May 1885).
34 Kemp (2004) pp. 7, 34.
35 Chambers, Spaenjers and Steiner (2021) p. 3592.

property, meaning that the College was intimately involved with the estate and the people living there, strengthening the social ties and sense of obligation as landowners.

Commercial property was not subject to these restrictions and was a more attractive proposition. But here the College had rather smaller holdings, partially because it had resisted the introduction of shops to the estate except in specific locations.[36] St John's did have some commercial property elsewhere, and quite a few farms, but as we saw above these were swamped by the value of the (almost entirely residential) property in Oxford. As well as being highly exposed to North Oxford, therefore, the College was particularly exposed to legislation affecting residential property. Following the Leasehold Reform Act 1967, property company Cluttons were commissioned to produce a report on the ideal property mix for the endowment and they advocated an allocation of 50 per cent commercial property (with another 25 per cent in agricultural land and 10 per cent in industrial property): the College's historical balance had been closer to 5 per cent.[37]

The picture was rather rosier when it came to the split within financial assets. Richardson was elected in 1951 and he set about stirring up change in the finances. As noted above, the first change was to the statutes governing the Trusts Fund: these were altered to allow investment in equities (at least in the larger firms). A few years later the statutes were changed again to include a statute explicitly dealing with investment, and the College's other funds could be invested in equities (subject to the existing limitations in law). A small but growing proportion

---

36 See for example SJC MUN V.C.10 (23 July 1860) limiting the number of shops allowed in Walton Manor.
37 SJC EST I.E.16 (Mar. 1969).

of the Trusts Fund began to be invested in equities, and when St John's gained the power to adjust its other endowments it did so rapidly, selling large amounts of gilts and buying equities in a variety of companies.

The argument was not won once for all.[38] In 1960 Sidney Ridley, the domestic bursar, pushed back with an investment memo: 'The question is whether the College, having derived a splendid advantage from the rise in the equity market in recent years, should not now consolidate its gains and take advantage of the present opportunity to invest in gilt-edge and similar securities.' His reasoning was that equities had risen but this return was in the form of capital gains, whereas the College wanted income. On top of that, the outlook for equities was uncertain; shifting into fixed income would guarantee the College a good level of income for the next decade or so. Richardson pushed back in committee: the aim was *not* to maximise income but to diversify so as to 'preserve our future income, in real terms, by hedging against a variety of possible circumstances. Sir Sidney considers the relative attractions of equities and gilt-edged in isolation, without any reference to the structure of our wealth as a whole.' Richardson felt there were two worrying future scenarios: depression and inflation. In the event of a depression the College's land would be a cushion; but if inflation came the fixed-income securities would suffer. The College was switching into equities to protect against this scenario. The rest of the committee, probably judging itself unable to adjudicate between the two theories, decided that advice should be sought from Scrimgeour, the College broker, and Geoffrey Kitchen of the Pearl Assurance company. They proceeded to repeat the same arguments that Richardson and Ridley, respectively, had

---

38 This paragraph is based on multiple documents in SJC ADM III.A.14.

advanced. Fortunately the College invited Scrimgeour to dinner and he had a chance to conclusively persuade them.

What was going on here? In part it was a clash of approaches to investment. George Richardson, the young economics don, saw investment through the lens of financial theory. His focus on 'the structure of our wealth as a whole' could have come straight from Markowitz, whether he had read his paper or not. Ridley, who was nearing retirement, had a more traditional focus. As domestic bursar he was responsible for the day-to-day running of the College and knew how important income from the endowment was. Equities were volatile: the College had made a gamble by moving into them and it had paid off handsomely; but wasn't it time to get back to the tried-and-tested gilts and take the profits? As we have seen, equity investment had only become relatively commonplace in institutions after the Second World War, and St John's had been less affected by that conflict than most. Steeped in an older way of doing things, where risk aversion and the preservation of capital were the watchwords, he probably felt there was much to value from that pre-war world.

From another perspective, however, the argument was about investment styles. No one – neither Ridley and Kitchen nor Richardson and Scrimgeour – thought that the College should or could dart around the market, sniffing out undervalued assets and investing in them, then flipping them when conditions changed. But this was nonetheless essentially what Ridley and Kitchen were recommending: the College had done well in equities; it could now get ahead of a coming change and get into bonds. The efficient markets hypothesis formalises the problem with this perspective: if you think that something is likely to become more valuable in the future – say you think, as Ridley did, that the economy is likely to take a turn for the worse and equity values will fall – then other people have probably realised that too and the information is already 'priced in'. The theory only became popular in finance in the 1960s, but like other principles, the intuition was already well known to many market participants: in his protests against the switch Scrimgeour wrote 'it was never the intention to endeavour to take advantage of short term market movements. Indeed, it is extremely difficult to do this.' What he and Richardson were advocating was an approach which *didn't* assume you had access to information the rest of the market lacked, but which would work in whatever situation the College found itself. Ridley's suggestion to move into 'safe' fixed-income products with a clear return seemed the sensible, cautious thing to do. In fact, it was Richardson's plan that was sensible and cautious: he didn't assume the College had the ability to play the market and designed a portfolio that reflected its needs and the threats it faced.

Interestingly, Keynes seems to have gone through a similar experience. Early on in his investing life, including in his investments for King's, he had tried to time the market and used active strategies. But he seems to have been unable to do so successfully, and after the Wall Street Crash in 1929 he changed his investment philosophy:

> As time goes on, I get more and more convinced that the right method in investment is to put fairly large sums into enterprises which one thinks one knows something about and in the management of which one thoroughly believes … The real limitation, however, on its application in practice is in my experience the small number of enterprises about which at any given time one feels in this way. One's knowledge and experience are definitely limited and there are seldom more than two or three enterprises at any given

time in which I personally feel myself entitled to put *full* confidence.[39]

This is not quite the same as Richardson and Scrimgeour, for Keynes did feel he had some special knowledge of the situation – but he makes it clear that this was due to research he had conducted and which was intensive enough that it could not be carried out for many enterprises.

Setting property aside, the reasons the College held the mix of assets it did is best explained not through portfolio theory but through a changing of the guard. Richardson, and the professionals he brought on board by encouraging a move into equities in the first place, conceptualised what the College portfolio was supposed to do in a fundamentally different way to how it had been seen before: one based on economic analysis rather than assumptions about what had always been done and the 'safety' this represented. Although resistance to such changes could be expressed in the language of different economic theories, it was not duelling theories which were at the root of the issue: it was a deeper set of differences in understanding the world. Ridley's advice to pre-empt the market was just the same as Hart-Synnot's method of predicting changes in the price level and trading accordingly so as 'to make a profit by switching over from one class to another'.[40] Fortunately Richardson's reforms were successful, and so this small part of the College's portfolio was left better able to deal with coming storms.

As we saw in Chapter 1, much of the reason that the College was invested in North Oxford comes down to it being lucky enough to have owned the land there when it became ripe for

---

39 Chambers, Dimson and Foo (2015b) pp. 852–3; Keynes (2013) p. 57.
40 SJC ADM III.B.7.

building. As St John's was restricted in selling endowed land and it was North Oxford which had made the College wealthy in the first place, that property naturally formed a disproportionate part of the overall portfolio. Furthermore, the scale of investment in property made sense when it was the only asset that could be held which would provide real growth over time, as land became more valuable because of growing cities or more productive farms. Hart-Synnot was clear about the issue: 'The College has found that the judicious purchase of real estate is the only means by which it can in ordinary circumstances provide for capital appreciation.'[41] To deal with this, the endowment was split between rack rents, ground rents, and trustee securities.

After the Second World War, however, opportunities for alternative forms of investment began opening up: holding on to North Oxford was still the default choice, but the College was beginning to recognise that this was still a *choice*. The Fellows had started to grasp something of the scale of the problem – Garrard wrote in a memo for Finance Committee that 'it is now being shown by revaluation that … [the] rents … are far from representing the value of the property and, to get a fairer picture, I propose to start a new register which will show the true rental value of each house and the money we actually receive.'[42] In other words, even the bursar did not have a good idea of how much the College's property portfolio was worth.

As we saw above, the answer, first delivered in 1961, was shocking. The College had become wealthy owing to North Oxford and it was still only wealthy because of North Oxford; take that away and it would be left with very little. Yet even a cursory view of the estate suggested that it was not an ideal asset for the College

---

41 SJC ADM III.B.7.
42 SJC ADM III.A.14.

to hold. And there was an additional problem: the College was vulnerable to political interference in its concentrated property.

We saw in Chapter 1 the form this political interference took: long leaseholds, which even in the 1950s were an important portion of the College's endowment income and represented about 45 per cent of its wealth, were reformed and their value plummeted. There had already been many changes in legislation throughout the century, and not all one way – in 1957 the Conservatives changed the law, allowing the College to raise rents across the estate – but collectively they made investment returns more uncertain and meant the College was especially vulnerable to a sudden change in the law. I explore the history of these restrictions and reforms in Chapter 3, but here we are interested in knowing what it implies for the College's choice of investments.

The standard solution to the exposure of one asset to political risk is simple: invest little bits of your endowment in many different securities, and then only some will be affected if the political risk is realised. You may not be able to eliminate the risk but you can make it relatively unimportant. It was this reasoning which Richardson identified in his memo and offered to Governing Body, and it was (initially) accepted. After all, it was a risk they were aware of, even if some experts played down the likelihood of it actually occurring. But then came the pressure to redevelop North Oxford.

Lords of the Manor

To reach Port Meadow – the western boundary of the College's North Oxford property – you can turn west off Walton Street in Jericho and go down a slightly inclined road towards the bridge. To your left are the old Eagle ironworks, now a canal-side apartment complex (St John's sold the freehold to the company in 1954).[43] And on your right is a small drinking fountain with an inscription noting that nearby was the source of 'a celebrated spring known as Walton Well'.[44] The inscription also states that the fountain was built in 1885 with the consent of the Lords of the Manor. Or to give them their full name: the President and Scholars of Saint John Baptist College in the University of Oxford.

As we saw in Chapter 1, the College had bought the lordships of manors around Oxford as investments. But land was never *just* a commodity in England, and owning it gave the Fellows a certain social cachet. In fact their connection to it could be much greater than that of aristocrats who also owned broad acres because, as an ecclesiastical corporation, the College also had the 'cure of souls' in many of the parcels of land it owned and was thus responsible for the spiritual welfare of the inhabitants. Even after the reforms of the mid-nineteenth century this was a responsibility taken seriously, with the President visiting parishes and recommending priests as late as the 1960s.[45] When it came to managing the North Oxford Estate – literally on the College's doorstep, and home to many of its Fellows and servants – it was even harder to see it as merely an investment. The temptation was to act in reality as they were legally: as lords of the manor.

That temptation does not seem to have been present at the beginning. To see as much, we must differentiate between

---

43 SJC EST I.A.18c (pp. 468–9).
44 This is not the only famous well nearby. If you cross Port Meadow and go to Binsey Church you will find in its graveyard St Margaret's Well, the waters of which the saint reportedly used to cure Algar's blindness. This was the inspiration for Lewis Carroll's Treacle Well (in Middle English 'treacle' meant an antidote against venom).
45 Mabbott (1986) pp. 129–31.

enlightened self-interest and charitable giving not designed to achieve a financial return. Planting a tree costs money now, but it will benefit many people later – and therefore their houses will be worth more. Enforcing covenants is expensive and time-consuming but it improves the overall character of the estate, meaning more money is collected overall. Not squeezing every last penny out of a tenant when you can raise rents loses you money now but gives you a reputation as an enlightened landlord and makes things easier in the future. All these sorts of trade-offs can be captured by the economic notion of externalities: the idea that something one person does imposes a cost or benefit on others which they do not consider. By owning the entire estate, rather than just a single house, the College was in a position to internalise those externalities and profit from its enlightened self-interest.

But you can always have too much of a good thing. Planting a few trees may well increase the value of the neighbourhood, but there comes a point when planting trees costs the College more than it gains in higher property values. Similarly, looking after your tenants will give you a good reputation, but at some point doing so is more costly than it is worth – at least in purely financial terms.

Initially the College seems to have been focused on financing the construction of the suburb in a way which would bring it good returns on a basis of enlightened self-interest. Covenants on the leases restricted the ability of leaseholders to keep horses that would smell, or sub-let to workshops that would lower the tone of the neighbourhood. Hinchcliffe describes the fight over building St Philip and St James Church – St John's did give some land and money for it, but the inhabitants also had to contribute (which they did not prove very willing to do, leading the priest to draft a letter lambasting them: 'Surely we have all freely received and have we so entirely to learn the precept "freely give"?').[46] Other factors look paternalistic – the church itself went through architectural, naming, and decorative changes to ensure it did not stray from High Anglican to Roman Catholic. (The silliest demand was probably that a scene of the crucifixion be replaced by one of Gethsemane: the cross apparently looked too much like a crucifix, suggestive of the Romish faith.) Similarly, when the College granted land to institutions such as Keble College, it came with conditions: Keble could not go over to the Church of Rome or the land would revert to St John's. But even these apparently religious interventions may be better explained as being about buttressing house prices, rather than bigotry – the dramatic events with St Philip and St James Church may have persuaded the Fellows that nearby houses might lose their value should those institutions shift their loyalty to Rome, and with a college named to honour a famous Tractarian that was no idle fear.

By the 1950s things were quite different. Managing the estate had been a great deal of work, as the vast number of complaints, enquiries, and gossip in the archives demonstrate. Probably the most ludicrous moment was when, in 1938, the Bursary prepared a notice for general circulation about pigeons. The document went through a series of increasingly inquisitorial questions – 'Do you own any pigeons, or allow them to be kept on your premises? Are pigeons not belonging to you being fed on your leasehold? Can you inform me of the name and address of any neighbouring owner of pigeons, with whom the College can get in touch?' – before ending on a supportive note: 'Have you experienced recently any annoyance from pigeons?'[47] But there were others: arguments about closing pubs, painting houses, altering leases,

---

46 Hinchcliffe (1992) p. 139.
47 SJC MUN V.C.52.

etc. Schools pestered the Bursary, hoping to buy their land at knock-down prices.[48] When the houses were not in the condition lessees wanted them to be on, they would complain to the local MP.[49] It took a firm personality to resist excessive claims, and Hart-Synnot and Garrard certainly provided that: the former was known for his letters to residents of North Oxford specifying how they were breaching their covenants (and causing them to complain to Fellows at North Oxford parties); we have seen how the latter handled challenges to rights of way on the College's land. They were not pushovers. But Garrard in particular felt the importance of the College's social obligations.

One example is when, following yet another change in rent control legislation, St John's was able to increase rents in 1957. Realising that this would be a challenge for many tenants, Garrard introduced a graduated increase over three years, which was often not up to the maximum the College could have gained. He set out the issues in his report:

> Obviously we cannot ask [this person] (or any other private resident) to pay over three times the present rent for her flat, even though Booth can produce six people, all of whom he suggests we should be delighted to have and would make excellent tenants. We ought to increase the rent, but to what figure? Knowing the true value to be £300, what principle is to guide us in raising the present rent from £81?[50]

Privately, he thought many of the government's restrictions were

---

48 SJC ADM II.C.2; SJC ADM II.B.20 (4 Mar. 1972).
49 SJC ADM III.C.30 (1963).
50 SJC ADM III.A.14.

inefficient and harmful, and when it came to businesses like farms he was more forceful:

> the Agriculture Act 1958 allows us to take a far tougher line with our tenants than has been possible for the last 20 years or so, and we can thus be more selective in our choice ... the poor and obstructive farmer we do not want. There are hundreds (literally) of good men waiting to start farming and one of the purposes of the new Act is to get them in and the others out.[51]

Privately, too, he complained about the 'storm of abuse ... by socialist members of the City Council ... In the campaign against the College exception has been taken more than once to a remark of mine: "... if they are living in houses they cannot afford, they will have to consider moving elsewhere." This is to me no more than a simple basic principle, but it is considered to be a "brutal" 20th Century equivalent of: "Qu'ils mangent de brioche."'[52] Publicly, however, he was restrained.

To some extent this is still enlightened self-interest: the College could not afford a fight with all its tenants. And, of course, the boundary between enlightened self-interest and charity is a subjective one. But there is reason to believe that Garrard crossed it. To get some elderly tenants out of their too-large houses, he gave a house to a society so that it could be used as an old people's home. There were financial benefits: securing 'vacant possession' of the houses they were in decontrolled them and allowed St John's to raise the rents they were charging. There were also social benefits: the women

---

[51] SJC ADM III.A.14.
[52] SJC ADM III.C.27.

Et in Arcadia Ego

all look years younger, have put on weight, and argue amongst themselves to their hearts' content. [One], aged 82, confessed (and there is no reason to doubt that she meant what she said) that at the time of the offer of a room in St. John's House she had been trying to pluck up enough courage to end it all in the gas oven, but that now she wanted for nothing, and hoped to live to be 120![53]

But there was a cost too: he went on to write that 'St. John's is not a philanthropic institution and it is expected that both projects will show a modest profit for the College.'[54] This sounds like enlightened self-interest: he explicitly claims the College is not engaging in philanthropy. But the concept of 'profit' here is in the accounting sense, not in the sense of getting the best possible return on assets. This was not unusual at the time, but it is a fundamentally different perspective to total return maximisation.[55]

Ultimately, Garrard was conflicted and recognised it. In his reports he discussed at length the importance of the College, as a tax-exempt landlord, setting a good example to other landlords. Despite recognising that the College's ownership of cottages was financially ridiculous (they brought in little rent and were very expensive to keep habitable) he made an exception for the cottages at Fyfield in south Oxforshire, which he wanted to become a 'Model Village, with the College taking a special interest in its

---

53 SJC ADM III.C.29.
54 SJC ADM III.C.29.
55 In 1961 the Estates Bursar at University College suggested setting up a fund that would allow richer colleges to contribute to poorer ones, essentially by exploiting the technical differences between income and capital. The fund would be legal because there would be an accounting profit but it would clearly not maximise the richer colleges' income.

appearance and in the well-being of the tenants'.[56] And yet even here he was cognisant of the financial needs of the College:

> There are few things that would interest me more than the reconditioning of all our cottages, but I know that the cost and return make such a project impossible. We cannot afford the £75,000 to £100,000. And could we justify the spending of College capital on modernising homes for workers in industry, who at the most, would pay us an uneconomic 12/- to 15/- a week, from a wage which is based, among other things, on a house rent of 25/- to 30/-? I suggest that the landlord of today is so much the butt of adverse legislation that he can no longer remain the traditional philanthropist of the countryside: and he <u>ought</u> not to. They cannot have it both ways. He <u>must</u> keep his farms up-to-date … also the cottages, so that those who work on the land may live in conditions of comfort at least comparable with those of their friends in the Towns. And that is as far as I think the College should go: except that I have been so inconsistent as to hope we may stay in Fyfield and do all the things I have tried to show we ought not to do.[57]

The planned redevelopment of North Oxford was even more extreme. From the start, the plan relied on support from the local council, but even with this support it was very unclear that it made financial sense for the College.[58] Throughout the

---

56 SJC ADM C.III.1 (1952 p. 6).
57 SJC ADM C.III.1 (1952 pp. 17–18).
58 The council was quite clear that it hadn't spent money on roads in Walton Manor before and wanted strong arguments for doing so – arguments which the College consistently failed to provide. Later Lord Esher wrote that the 'village feel' created by the road widening was an objective that had 'always been shared by the City

planning they were told that, whatever people like Lord Harcourt claimed, the area was *not* 'ripe for redevelopment' and that the existing houses were probably worth more standing than the empty plots would be. And to finance the project the College had to hold on to their estate and put in more money by buying in leases, rather than divesting and acquiring more suitable assets. Here the urge to be lord of the manor – developing an ideal village for tenants; micromanaging the community; planning everything from the centre – was given full rein. In the end it was disastrous.

One important question is whether the College *could* have offloaded its Oxford property: there is only so much demand for property in one area at any one time, and releasing more onto the market can have the effect of depressing prices. I investigate this in more detail in Chapter 5, but the evidence from other institutions suggests that St John's could have withdrawn quite a lot of its capital. Similarly, alternative paths existed when it came to lobbying against leasehold reform – a great many institutions did, some quite successfully – and redeveloping urban property. It was a case of wouldn't rather than couldn't.

Accounting for Failure

What went wrong with the College's portfolio in the 1950s and 60s? The move from fixed income to equities was actually quite rapid and successful, once it was finally under way, and despite challenges to the policy the College persisted in it. (As we saw in Chapter 1, the actual investments chosen were not so successful,

---

Authorities and by the College, and [was] certainly not in the financial interests, or I would think even the capacity, of the College without the City's help.' SJC MUN V.C.67.3.

but this is not a criticism of the overall strategy.) But the good effect of this change was dwarfed by the damage done by holding an excessive amount of real estate, leading both to a bad asset mix and massive losses following leasehold enfranchisement.

The immediate responsibility for this must lie with Garrard. After Governing Body decided to divest from North Oxford, Garrard did align himself with the new policy on paper. But he never seems to have done so in spirit – probably because he liked intervening in the disputes and superintending the repairs and generally running the estate. This is not to say, of course, that he defied Governing Body. It is just that the situation was not treated as urgent – to the extent that, two years after Governing Body had resolved to sell large swathes of the estate, so much remained that they could discuss a counter-proposal to redevelop a large part of it and fund that redevelopment by selling other parts of it! Any collegiate decision, once made, needs someone to push it through: as bursar, Garrard should have been that man.

But this is only the proximate cause. After Governing Body had approved the redevelopment plan, Garrard sent a short letter to Lionel Brett (later Lord Esher), the architect tasked with redesigning Walton Manor: 'At last the College have reached agreement on the North Oxford Estate. We are not going to sell as recommended in the Joint Report of 1960 because the Economists are now persuaded that we should do better in the long run by hanging on.'[59] Responsibility must indeed lie, not just with Richardson who was persuaded to recant, but the entire Governing Body. Ultimately, they were the ones who decided what to do. They could have instructed Garrard to move faster if necessary. Furthermore, they were responsible for the appointment of

---

59 SJC MUN V.C.66 (9 Oct. 1962).

Et in Arcadia Ego

Garrard, and then Harry Kidd, as bursar in the first place. Both were capable men committed to serving St John's, but neither was an expert in investments or the management of an urban estate, although this represented the overwhelming majority of the College's endowment. From this perspective both men were (unintentionally) set up for failure.

To some extent this was a result of the dons not taking enough consideration of the College's situation. It was easy to believe that the College was rich and would remain so – other people were paid to think about the details. We have seen that many members of Finance Committee didn't really feel qualified to decide between the different investment policies presented by Richardson and Ridley. But they also liked being lords of the manor. As Neild wrote about the Fellows of Trinity College, Cambridge: 'the dons took pleasure in thinking of themselves as rural landlords. They took pride in the possession of "foundation land"; they might look forward – or backward – to days spent shooting over a college farm and being entertained to lunch by the tenant.'[60] There was an attitude of benevolent paternalism towards the estate and its residents.

But this was out of step with the political reality of the situation. In 1855, when the College began building North Oxford, St John's was at the edge of the city. A century later, North Oxford was under the jurisdiction of the city council. When the College was building the suburb, it had to put in roads and sewers at its own expense; a century later these were handled by the city council. And in 1855 it was up to the College to plan what would be built where and in which forms; a century later the city council was engaging in slum clearance and had a plan for relief roads. It is possible that the University's success

---

60 Neild (2012) p. 21.

in getting the latter killed gave St John's too strong an opinion of its own ability to control policy, but it should have realised that it did not have the financial resources to engage in even a relatively small redevelopment without the council's financial support. Bigger projects such as renovating the working-class cottages in the west were recognised to be beyond its power. And although the College did stay in touch with the council, they often seem to have heard what they wanted to hear, rather than what the council was really saying.

This failure to recognise and engage with power on a local level was replicated on a national scale when leasehold reform occurred. The White Paper published by the Labour government after it won the General Election in 1964 set out the confiscatory nature of the plan. But it was not implemented until 1967, following another election in 1966. Other landowners lobbied against it and secured important changes (discussed in Chapter 5). But all St John's did was try to avoid the impact of the law by setting up a housing association – a tactic so unsuccessful that the government, after getting wind of the scheme, specifically changed the draft legislation to prevent it.[61] They did not join similar institutions such as the Church Commissioners or Eton College, or the great families like the Grosvenors who also owned large estates, in (with some success) lobbying the government. Unlike Trinity and St John's colleges in Cambridge, they did not submit any notes or arguments to the Ministry of Housing and Local Government. When Dr Radcliffe's School got in touch to say that they were in a similar situation and wanted to join forces, Garrard responded that St John's wasn't interested and were waiting to see the text of the Bill.[62] Eleven

---

61 NA HLG 29/734.
62 SJC EST I.M.Main.318 (4 and 10 Oct. 1966).

Et in Arcadia Ego

years later, Trinity College, Cambridge would manage to kill a Bill that would have semi-nationalised Felixstowe Dock, the source of much of its wealth, at its last stage in the Lords.[63] So it was not necessarily the case that St John's could not have lobbied effectively (although of course it was a different situation). Instead the College acted like an ostrich: burying its head in the sand, and scratching about with ineffectual plans to avoid the oncoming danger.

None of this is to deny that there were very real roadblocks in the College's way when it came to implementing Governing Body's 1960 resolution to divest from North Oxford. The need to create sinking funds when it sold property did make divestment less attractive than it would otherwise have been, although given the extent of the College's exposure significant divestment still made sense. In a memo following a meeting with Major Dobb at the ministry, Garrard noted that he had

> complained to Major Dobb that we were being frustrated in our efforts to help other Colleges in their reasonable expansion by his Ministry's refusal to sanction sales where the Sinking Fund was fixed so high that the College would be worse off financially after selling than before. He agreed that this sounded ridiculous and undertook to try to find a solution. Major Dobb gave every indication that he was anxious to help and to rectify the impression of obstructiveness created by his colleagues in the Ministry.[64]

One could question whether this was the right area for help – the problem was that St John's was disposing of property to

---

63 Neild (2008) p. 128.
64 SJC ADM II.C.3 (4 Oct. 1960).

other colleges at below-market prices – but it does confirm that it was an issue and that the Ministry had, historically, not been helpful.

Another problem was the Ministry of Agriculture's conservative approach to even entirely sensible financial solutions. One obvious response to the problem of having too much exposure to property in one area would be to create a company that owned the estate and then sell shares in that. Doing so would allow the College to fine-tune its exposure while allowing all the shareholders to continue to benefit from internalising the externalities in the estate – at least the ones which remained. But when the College proposed something a bit like this the Ministry shot them down: 'The suggestion that the College might form a property development company jointly with a group of insurance companies had been considered and in the opinion of Mr. David such a scheme would not be approved by the Minister.'[65] By the time the Ministry's control ended in 1964 it was too late (although a similar scheme was proposed in 1967).[66] That the College was thinking about such schemes was a positive sign, but it reinforces the point that it was a failure to carry through the ideas Richardson had presented which was responsible for the financial disaster which hit the College.

Conclusion

The College's portfolio problem can be analysed in terms of financial theory, and it was this analysis that led to it changing in the 1950s and 60s and becoming closer to the portfolio we observe today. But it was not that an ideal portfolio was

---

65 SJC ADM III.A.15 (11 Jan. 1961).
66 SJC MUN V.C.67 iii (6 Dec. 1967).

repeatedly calculated and then transactions were made until the endowment resembled it. Instead, fairly basic analysis revealed two major problems: the asset mix underweighted equities; and there was enormous exposure to real estate in North Oxford. Neither of these issues could be easily changed, owing to a combination of legal restrictions, conservative attitudes in the College, and simple inertia. Thanks to a sustained lobbying effort from Richardson progress was made on both these problems – but whereas the asset diversification project was able to resist attempts to backtrack, the North Oxford divestment project was not. The difference between the two was that moving from gilts into equities, while a break with the past, did not involve any serious emotional work: gilts and equities were both investments and, even if there were concerns about the risks involved in equities, they were clearly both technologies designed to achieve the same ends (albeit in different ways and with different emphases *among* those aims). But land and an estate were not merely financial technologies for transforming present purchasing power into future purchasing power. This was just the tip of a social iceberg of status, responsibility, and charity. Breaking that link was a much harder wrench than selling off gilts to buy equities – as late as 1969 property consultants hired by the College explicitly excluded the village of Fyfield (to which the Founder had retired and which the College owned) from their analysis, noting that it certainly didn't make sense as part of the portfolio but the Fellows had a historic attachment to it.[67]

And the link meant that when pressure was put on the College to fulfil its social role and redevelop North Oxford for the good of the city and University – although not its own good

---

67 SJC EST I.E.16.

Intellectual Capital

– the pressure was too great. Sensible portfolio management was out; a risky bet against leasehold enfranchisement was in. Just how risky will be explored in the next chapter.

3

THE AVALANCHE

Could Anyone Have Seen Leasehold Reform Coming?

> The inhabitants of Oxford are not in the world and when they do sally forth into the world (to London, for example) that in itself is enough to have them gasping for air; their ears buzz, they lose their sense of balance, they stumble and have to come scurrying back to the town that makes their existence possible, that contains them, where they do not even exist in time.
>
> J. Marías, All Souls, 1992

In 1965, F. M. L. Thompson noted a curious fact about the social reform movements of the nineteenth century. All the reasonable ones had succeeded – apart from land reform. Its failure meant that it had to be classed with 'republicanism, teetotalism, and disestablishmentarianism, yet in its day it was a movement worthy of more than such cranky associates'.[1] One might imagine that the Leasehold Reform Act 1967 and its progeny would have changed his mind, but this is not the case:

---

1 Thompson (1965) p. 23.

he repeated substantially the same arguments in 2010.² There is a consensus that land reform, while an important movement up to the First World War, was subsequently neutered because land reform had never really been about reforming land ownership for the sake of reforming land ownership. Instead it was about targeting the aristocracy who were large landowners.³ As the power of the aristocracy declined after the First World War and their land ownership decreased, there ceased to be much of a point in advocating for land reform.

Was land reform merely a stalking horse for class warfare? A persuasive case has been made that this was part of the story. Support for reform *did* drop off significantly after the First World War, and this coincided with higher death duties and other measures which negatively impacted the aristocracy. Political support *was* lacking: the first Liberal Land Campaign, advocating a land value tax (in the spirit of Henry George), had seen mass popular support, whereas when Lloyd George attempted a second in 1926 it was 'a flop'.⁴ After its success in having the Corn Laws abolished, the Anti-Corn Law League considered turning its attention to land reform.

But there are problems with this view, and the Leasehold Reform Act 1967 highlights them. There were real issues with the legal form some tenancies took. There was persistent anger about inequality in land ownership and the power this gave individuals and institutions. And there was, of course, the Act

---

2 Thompson in Cragoe and Readman (2010).
3 See for example Quinault in Cragoe and Readman (2010) pp. 177–8: 'The urban land reform campaign was a failure before the First World War and during the inter-war period it died as a major political movement. Yet it left a legacy ... the 1967 Leasehold Enfranchisement Act [sic.] ... belatedly implemented a measure that London reformers had hoped to enact in the 1880s.'
4 Thompson in Cragoe and Readman (2010) p. 259.

itself: a dramatic legislative intervention that tore many estates away from their owners and literally reshaped the urban landscape in many cities. So what have historians missed?

Reasons for Reform

If the arguments actually advanced for land reform – that the existing system entrenched inequality by giving the wealthy an 'unearned increment', encouraged inefficiency by working against a free market in land, and allowed for abuse of market power by landowners who were effectively monopolists – were specious, then contemporaries should have realised this and pointed it out. (The 'unearned increment' was the idea that landowners benefited from rising land prices even if they had done nothing to cause that increase in value: for example the land that became North Oxford was valuable because the city had grown, but St John's had not played much of a role in making the city grow.) To some extent this did happen – Thompson has written about how primogeniture (the custom that the eldest son inherited the lands, thus keeping large estates intact) was 'clearly the paper dragon, a thing of no importance in itself, but an unfailing red rag to the landowners, and a slogan or war-chant to rally the great dispossessed'.[5] When it was finally abolished in 1925 very little changed. But other complaints and suggested reforms were much more reasonable. There are still concerns that unearned benefits accrue to landowners who happen to have land in the right places today and that this frustrates development and economic equity.[6]

Furthermore, many of the issues raised in regard to the

---

5 Thompson (1965) p. 34.
6 Collier (2018) pp. 63–7.

problems with leasehold did end up causing difficulties later on, and eventually received legislative attention: the Leasehold Reform Act 1967 is the standout example but, as we will see in Chapter 5, similar issues continue today. This suggests that much of what was being protested about was both insightful and correct. At the very least, it demonstrates that it was a political issue that would outlive specific challenges to the landed aristocracy.

Perhaps the problem is that too much has been expected from land reform. If it was about overthrowing the aristocracy and redrawing patterns of land ownership root and branch across the length and breadth of this sceptred isle, then certainly it was a failure. On the other hand, if the reformers and protesters merely wanted to incrementally improve their life circumstances, then much of the history of the post-First World War housing market – rent control, leasehold reform giveaways, the growth of social housing – can be seen as a series of short-term successes (albeit marred by long-term stagnation). From this perspective the battle is over housing: rural reform would be a nice cherry but urban reform is the cake. Thus leasehold reform and rent control become part of the same tradition of protest and political critique as other types of land reform. Leasehold reform should be seen as an aspect of land reform.

And yet the belief that land reform ceased to be relevant doesn't altogether fly in the face of the evidence. As I noted above, agitation on behalf of land reform declined after the First World War. And yet access to housing remained an important political flashpoint. In 1915, the Rents and Mortgage Interest Restriction Act was introduced to restrict the ability of landlords to raise rents as workers flooded into the cities to support war production. Because it also froze mortgage interest rates, many landlords also benefited from it – so despite it being pitched as a temporary measure, attempts to remove rent and mortgage control led to political opposition. In 1923, the ruling Conservatives commissioned the Onslow Report to decide what to do; but when they tried to follow its recommendation of decontrolling tenancies they lost three by-elections in safe seats in a row and were scared off. Rent control continued until 1988, albeit with regular changes as governments succeeded each other. Housing did not leave the political agenda, and for many renters – especially those living in the growing number of council houses – land reform may not have seemed an especially important concern because the power of private landowners was so trammelled.

Debate within the Labour Party reflected this. There was disagreement over the correct socialist policy position: should houses be owned by the state (perhaps locally, i.e., municipalisation); or should each house be owned by its own household, i.e., owner-occupation? Ortolano has shown that as a result Labour governments ended up supporting both options, providing funds for council housing but also sometimes offering mortgages.[7] Thus, despite underlying disagreement about what the true socialist state would look like, in practice Labour was focused on delivering housing outcomes which people would be sufficiently satisfied with.

All this is to say that there are multiple potential perspectives on the issue of land reform, reflecting the multiple forms of tenure and investment represented in twentieth-century Britain. And for the leaseholders who benefited from the change – especially those who argued for it on the basis of a moral grievance against the freeholders – it was doubtless a very significant change as well. Leasehold reform, therefore, is worth

---

7 Ortolano (2021) p. 322.

studying in its own right; it also reveals more about Labour's policy towards land reform and housing in this period and the subsequent development of the situation in Britain.

A Changing Political Situation

In the previous chapter, I noted that when St John's began to build North Oxford the city council played a relatively minor role. The College organised the covenants on the leases dictating the design of the houses, and pushed back on architects who transgressed against their plan for building zones for different classes of tenant.[8] Roads, sewers, and even telegraph lines were organised by the College.[9] But this was beginning to change even before the turn of the century, as the city took over the responsibility for roads; and other powers followed. By 1960 the shoe was on the other foot: the city council was more powerful, both financially and politically, than the College. And what was true in Oxford was broadly true throughout the nation (although, as we will see in Chapter 5, some landowners such as the Grosvenors were able to wield significant political power). The result was that many of the benefits provided by a single landowner could equally be provided by local government – and there was a growing sense that this was the democratically legitimate way to provide them. Before building, an estate might have consisted of unpopulated fields, but communities grew up in them and had a stake in what happened to them, becoming an alternative source of legitimacy. Both politically and financially, therefore, the stage was set for a very different kind of negotiation between lessor and lessee when long leases began to fall in.

---

8 Hinchcliffe (1992) pp. 81–2.
9 For example SJC MUN V.C.13.

The Avalanche

There was already reason to believe that these negotiations would be fraught. Long leases were not scattered uniformly around Britain – historically they were concentrated where an estate had chosen to use them to maintain its integrity and control. In other areas, often because of greater competition among potential lessors due to fragmented land ownership, freehold (sometimes with covenants and an annual rent charge) or 999-year leases were more common.[10] The 99-year lease had been pioneered by the Duke of Bedford in 1774 when he was building areas of Bloomsbury (especially Bedford Square in 1776), and London remained an area with significant numbers of long leaseholds, along with Oxford and Liverpool. But by far the most incendiary situation was in Wales.[11] In Cardiff, for example, the Butes had owned much of the land and were responsible for developing the docks which made the city (and the family) wealthy, and many tenants had only been given the option of a 99-year lease.[12] As aristocratic fortunes diminished, the Butes joined other families in selling their freeholds: in 1938 Western Ground Rents, a name that would become infamous, bought a large parcel of Cardiff land from the Butes.[13] The company had been set up specifically for the transaction, and was financed by insurance companies who wanted to invest in property.

The transaction broke the historical continuity of the Butes' ownership of, and service to, the city. This may not have meant very much: they were not immune to the changing economic and political circumstances, and whereas the second marquess – who had decided to develop the docks – had dominated

---

10 Davey (2006) p. 152.
11 Cannadine (1980) pp. 15, 31; Quinault (2010) p. 172.
12 Davies (1981) pp. 188–9, 246–7.
13 Hinchcliffe (2017) pp. 114–15.

Cardiff politics and its corporation, the third marquess felt he was elected as mayor 'as a kind of figurehead, and although they are good enough to be glad whenever I take part in details, I am willing to leave those in the hands of people with more expertise than myself'.[14] The newly confident corporation even tried to take over the docks.[15] Nevertheless, leaseholders frustrated with their situation could now point to a faceless investment company rather than a storied family when airing their grievances. And there were many grievances.

The Economics of Leases

Leaseholders had been frustrated with their situation for a long time. There are inherent problems with a long lease on residential property. First, it reduces the lessee's control over their home through covenants. This can be valuable – if nearby houses have similar controls the character of the neighbourhood is preserved – but it is frustrating, and as time went on, it seemed less and less politically acceptable.

Second, lessees were responsible for paying 'dilapidations' at the end of the lease: the idea was that the house would be returned to the lessor in the condition it had been built in. In principle, this was unproblematic; in practice, unscrupulous lessors would demand fees for unreasonable adjustments. These demands were nothing more than a shakedown, and discouraged investment in the property during the lease. Such investment was further discouraged by the lessor's ability to charge a fee for modifications to the house even when these were completed at the tenant's expense and would add value.

---

14 Cannadine (1980) pp. 41, 56.
15 Ibid. p. 50.

The Avalanche

Sometimes both issues would arise: in 1953 the House of Lords heard how, when

> a lessee was anxious to carry out improvements to his premises ... for instance, the putting in of a second bathroom ... he had to agree to an increased rent because of the greater value of the premises. He also had to agree to restore the premises at the end of the lease to the condition in which they were; in other words, to take away the second bathroom – not that the landlord would want him to do so, but it was a lever with which to extract, if he could, a bigger sum in respect of dilapidations.[16]

The Landlord and Tenant Act 1927 attempted to deal with this issue but provided insufficient compensation for improvements, and it was cumbersome for tenants while being easy for landlords to circumvent.[17] Not all lessors engaged in these practices, but the freehold was more valuable to those that were willing to do so, and so there was some reason to believe that bad managers would drive out good – a concern strengthened after aristocratic sales led to the owners of freeholds being more distant from the community. In the debate on the doomed Leasehold Reform Bill in 1962 Alan Glyn MP expressed the same concern: 'most of the good, large estates were owned by people who showed a reasonable attitude towards their tenants. For one reason and another that is not true today. All over the country we are getting what I make no apology to the House for describing as "spiv" landlords coming in.'[18]

---

16 *Hansard*. HL Deb. Vol. 180 Col. 519 (18 Feb. 1953).
17 Haley (1991) p. 122.
18 *Hansard*. HC Deb. Vol. 668 Col. 1679 (7 Dec. 1962).

Third, long leaseholds provided little financial benefit and set lessees up for regret. The value of a freehold can be construed as the discounted stream of rents it is capable of bringing in (adjusting for uncertainty, potential redevelopment and associated costs, etc.). From this perspective, a lease is just a temporally bounded subset of the benefits from a property, and it is simple to calculate its value. A capital-constrained buyer might prefer the lease because the price is lower. Long leases also came with a periodic ground rent which was effectively a form of financing for the lessee akin to a mortgage: the lessee paid less upfront and paid off the additional 'debt' gradually, with the remainder of the lease as security. This analysis is persuasive for someone agreeing to rent a house for a year but not for 99-year leases in the way they operated in Britain. For one thing, the present value of a house ninety-nine years hence is tiny given typical interest rates: at 5 per cent it is less than 1 per cent of the purchase price, and even at 2 per cent it is only about 14 per cent. Buyers were therefore saving an insignificant amount. Similarly ground rents were typically low, and thus did not represent a significant loan from the lessor to the lessee. The result was that a family would pay close to the freehold price for a long lease, spend a century making minimal payments, perhaps passing the property down through the generations – and then face a situation where they no longer had a right to live in the property. In fact it was worse than this, because the reversion value the freeholder held appreciated rapidly towards the end of the lease and the value of the lease correspondingly depreciated rapidly. This meant that selling the lease if you wanted to move elsewhere was difficult because banks were unwilling to secure a mortgage against the lease.[19] Although legislation was passed to ensure

---

19 Cmnd. 2916 quoted in NA HLG 29/723 (18 Feb. 1966) pp. 196–7.

that tenants could remain in the physical structure (unless the landlord wanted to redevelop it), it would be on much worse financial terms than they were used to. Given the emotional attachment people have to their home, it is difficult to see how the slight initial saving was anything but a Faustian pact.

And even the term 'pact' is misleading. A fourth issue was that many landowners had a monopoly over local land and could set their terms: if they wanted to offer only leasehold then there was nothing tenants could do about it. In a suburb like North Oxford this was not so significant – there were other places to live if you needed to be near Oxford, although they may not have been as nice or convenient – but if you needed work and the docks in Cardiff were your best option, then you had little choice. This had been recognised for a long time: the 1889 Report of the Select Committee on Town Holdings found that 'This feeling [of injustice at the end of the lease] is probably especially strong in cases where working men and others build their own homes and where, being unable to obtain land, either as freehold or long leasehold, they are practically compelled to build on leases for short terms', and the principle naturally extends to any non-freehold form of property.[20] Workers were not blind to the disadvantages of leasehold property and seem to have opted for freehold where they could: as we saw above, cities where land ownership was not so concentrated tended to have relatively fewer long leases. Lessees could point to objections to monopolies elsewhere in the economy and argue that they, too, had been victimised by lessors wielding excessive market power.

While some landlords benefited from their monopoly power, others might have been happy to sell freeholds had the law allowed it. The restrictions on colleges discussed in Chapter

---

20 Quoted in *Hansard*. HL Deb. Vol. 180 Col. 514 (18 Feb. 1953).

2, and similar restrictions imposed on many aristocratic estates, meant that long leaseholds were their only option if they had land that could be developed into urban property. Alan Glyn, who had complained about the 'spiv' landlords, raised this point during the same debate:

> if we look into history we find that the only forms of investment open to trusts were Government stock ... land and property. Those were the restrictions that so many estates had placed upon them until the Trustee Acts recently released them. They were, therefore, bound to invest in this type of property ... Had they been able to invest in other interests, their capital would have been protected and probably have increased in value.[21]

Taken together with the presence of land monopolies, this explains why the long leases (at least as they were set up in practice) made so little financial sense: that was not really the reason they were offered. And since many of the original constrained lessors had already sold up, there was even less sympathy for the owners of the freeholds who had chosen to invest in that type of asset. Furthermore, revisions to the restrictions on trustees meant that there was less reason to protect the ability of landlords to offer new leaseholds.

Long leaseholds made little financial sense, discouraged productive investment, encouraged abuse, were sometimes imposed on tenants because of arguably unjust concentrations of market power, and had by the mid-twentieth century lost their traditional justifications. Structurally, the stage was set for reform, although the precise parameters were always going to be subject

---

21 *Hansard*. HC Deb. Vol. 668 Col. 1677 (7 Dec. 1962).

to negotiation and a function of who held political power. Observers, such as the Fellows of St John's College, might not have been expected to take note of these underlying issues. But there were clearer signs that things were changing as well.

Populist Pressure

Land has been a perennial issue in British politics: the idea of the 'Norman yoke' had been around since the Civil War and was taken up by the Chartists in the 1840s.[22] Specific problems of dispossession in Ireland, Scotland, and Wales periodically rocked Westminster politics. More generally, the reforms advocated by Henry George (a prominent American who pushed for a land value tax) and J. E. Thorold Rogers (a political economist at Oxford) were popular and backed by reams of data on the very concentrated nature of land ownership in Britain. Concerns about urban property, however, only became a focus later on. The issue may well have risen to prominence because urbanisation was increasing rapidly in this period – from about 40 per cent in the 1840s to 70 per cent in the 1890s – which both made the issue more salient for more of the population, and worsened conditions in cities as the rate of house building failed to keep pace and new arrivals found themselves crammed into houses with multiple families.[23] The situation was bad enough that a Royal Commission on the Housing of the Working Classes was set up, and most members felt that leasehold enfranchisement would help by discouraging bad building.[24]

The first sign that the status of leaseholds might not be

---

22 Chase (2010) p. 59.
23 Davenport (2020) pp. 456–7; Englander (1983) pp. x–xi.
24 Davey (1994) p. 774.

completely safe came in 1883, just before the Commission's report, when the Leasehold Enfranchisement Association was set up. Leasehold Enfranchisement bills began to follow in Parliament; these never gained sufficient support but were an early sign that the issue might divide parties and attract politicians who scented the possibility of a popular giveaway. For example, when such a Bill was introduced in 1885 by Henry Broadhurst, a radical Liberal MP, much of the Liberal Party was against it; in 1891 the Fabians persuaded them to vote another one down, on the grounds that it would reinforce property and discourage the ultimate goal of land nationalisation.[25] There was similar dissent among the Conservatives: Randolph Churchill, arguing that spreading ownership throughout the population was a conservative idea, put forward a Bill in 1884, but it did not find favour with his party's leadership (possibly owing to Lord Salisbury's ownership of valuable land in central London).[26] Attempts in the same vein continued, though never attracting enough support across the spectrum. In 1913 Lloyd George came out in support of leasehold reform, and had it not been for the First World War perhaps more progress would have been made. But even as he fell in behind the banner of reform, his Cabinet failed to join him.[27]

The pressure to reform leaseholds did not disappear after the First World War, but it was weakened. Rural land was still the focus: the Liberals published the 'Green Book' and 'Brown Book', with the former – focused on rural land reform – getting more attention.[28] The Brown Book had a chapter specifically

---

25 Offer (1981) p. 157.
26 Quinault (2010) p. 172.
27 Ibid. p. 175.
28 Thompson (2010) p. 266.

on leaseholds and rehearsed many of the same arguments: landlords benefit from an unearned increment created by the tenant; properties near the end of the lease get run down; the fines and dilapidations are abused by lessors (including at least one, unnamed, Oxford college); there was often a monopoly when the leases were established which was especially unfair in Wales.[29] They called for leasehold enfranchisement but did not suggest principles by which the price would be set.[30] Another part of the explanation of why leasehold reform had, up to this point, played a minor role in land reform is that, with restrictions on rent increases, many people were protected: leasehold was a sideshow compared to the rental sector.

There was one worrying sign for estates, although we can hardly blame their administrators for not recognising it at the time. In 1920 the Places of Worship (Enfranchisement) Act was passed. It allowed for specific sites, mainly churches and chapels, to be purchased if they had been leased for twenty-one years or more. If compensation was disputed, an arbiter was to be set up by the judge of the county court. The Act further stated that 'In determining the amount of any compensation the value of any buildings erected, or improvements made by the trustees, shall be excluded.'[31] The Act was limited, but something like the principle that the freeholder only had an interest in what was on the land when the lease began – perhaps only the land itself – had been established.

The Brown Book's proposals were not implemented; the Liberals would not return to power. By accident rather than design, the country had stumbled into rent controls which

---

29 Liberal Land Committee (1925) pp. 4–5, 49–52, 60–61, 66.
30 Ibid. p. 158.
31 Places of Worship (Enfranchisement) Act (1920) 2 (c).

would characterise much of the twentieth century. It is easy to see why historians have concluded that the First World War sounded the death knell for leasehold enfranchisement. Events up to the 1960s sound blandly technocratic: the Landlord and Tenant Act 1927 (a feeble change to the tenant's ability to carry out improvements); the Leasehold Property (Repairs) Act 1938 (which restricted landlords' ability to enforce repairs despite the covenants in the lease); the 1950 minority report from the Jenkins Committee (it advocated leasehold enfranchisement, but the majority report did not); the Leasehold Property (Temporary Provisions) Act 1951 (which extended expiring leaseholds by two years until a solution could be found, but which, when no solution was found, itself had to be extended for eighteen months); and the Landlord and Tenant Act 1954 (the Conservatives' response to the majority report from the Jenkins Committee, giving some 'security of tenure' by allowing the tenant to stay in the property – but at the normal rent and not if the freeholder wanted to redevelop).

But still waters run deep. The reforms had improved the lessees' position, but not drastically. All the old complaints – complaints founded either on a sense of injustice or on real economic problems caused by long leaseholds – remained. And St John's had not been the only institution, benefiting from the growth of urbanisation, to build in the mid-nineteenth century. By the 1960s those leases were falling in; entirely predictable tensions were growing.[32] Rumours that the Labour Party, out of power but hungry for it, might be considering a populist giveaway to leaseholders began to circulate. Leasehold enfranchisement was Party policy: the 1961 conference had endorsed *Signposts for the Sixties* which stated 'More must be done to make

---

32 *Hansard*. HC Deb. Vol. 644 Col. 421–2 (12 July 1961).

it easier for people – including the tenants of private landlords – to buy their own homes ... We must also reform leasehold law to enable leaseholders with long leases to buy their own homes.'[33] *Country Life* worried that Labour's proposals for land nationalisation, which *Signposts for the Sixties* also endorsed, 'offer generous scope for criticism: their administrative difficulties, for instance, would appear to be formidable. But they are not to be underestimated. For politicians skilled in the drafting of electoral manifestos might present them in a manner attractive to an electorate rendered restless by a continuance of spectacular deals in land and property.'[34] *Country Life* was hardly an objective commentator, but its concern that the proposals were popular but badly thought through was prophetic.

Labour took power in 1964, narrowly defeating the Conservatives who had governed for thirteen years. With a majority of just four seats, Prime Minister Harold Wilson was in no position to resist his party's special interests – and James Callaghan, now Chancellor and representing Cardiff South East, was interested in leasehold enfranchisement. The ministry responsible for drawing up a plan was Housing, and it was now run by Richard Crossman.

Crossman is an interesting and not especially pleasant figure. He had been a Classics tutor at New College and was responsible for getting Isaiah Berlin his first post in Oxford. Berlin was clearly grateful and corresponded with Crossman throughout his life. But in private he let his conflicted feelings about the man show: 'Crossman really is a queer problem. He is not a good or admirable man, but he has been apparently both brave and right in the immediate past, how I am not sure; it is worthy

---

33 The Labour Party (1963) p. 22.
34 *Country Life* (14 Sept. 1961) p. 544.

of a first-rate psychological political novel, better than Koestler and not as good as Dostoevsky, about the level of Malraux I should say.'[35] Berlin was not alone in his assessment. At Winchester, Crossman had made it clear that he was unimpressed by the 'innocuous and insignificant' Hugh Gaitskell, which rather complicated things when Gaitskell was leader of the Labour Party.[36] The same criticism extended to his mother, for whom he would lay 'intellectual traps' over dinner: his cruelty resulted in the breakdown of his relationship not just with his father but also with their family friends, the Attlees, who 'never forgave me for causing my parents so much pain'.[37] His entry into politics may have been due to the advice of a friend to do it while he was young – but it may have been because his affair with a colleague's wife would have led to him being forced out of New College anyway.[38]

We know a lot about Crossman's time in the Cabinet because he kept a diary (which was remarkably candid – he revealed that he had perjured himself in a court case). From this we can see that he approached the question of leasehold reform in character. From the start he was annoyed with it, later describing it as an 'appalling political embarrassment' that he tried to hand off to another ministry.[39] His Parliamentary Private Secretary revealed that 'what appalled him was not the Civil Service but our own Labour Party housing specialists ... the housing cupboard was bare ... Precious little work had been done by the party on ... the means of redeeming much-trumpeted electoral promises.'[40] He

---

35 Berlin, Letter to Ursula Niebuhr (5 Mar. 1949) in Berlin (2011) p. 79.
36 Honeyman (2007) p. 17.
37 Ibid. pp. 17–18.
38 Ibid. p. 20.
39 Crossman (27 June 1965) in Crossman (1975) p. 256.
40 Dalyell (1989) pp. 114–15.

was more interested in a Bill on the Land Commission, but 'the Welsh pressure group led by Jim Callaghan and Jim Griffiths' meant that leasehold enfranchisement was prioritised.[41]

It does seem to have been true that, having promised voters and Welsh MPs *something*, the government was very unclear about what it could actually do. The situation was especially bad because MPs campaigning in 1964, aided by a Party document entitled *Speaker's Notes*, had extended the principle of enfranchisement from private property to public property and 'the Welsh candidates, headed by James Callaghan and James Griffiths, had promised virtual confiscation of all long leases in South Wales and the same promises have been made in Birmingham.'[42] But Crossman was opposed on socialist grounds to the application of enfranchisement to public property. This must have been intensely frustrating for his colleagues. Fred Willey, the Minister for Housing, had prepared a Bill that adopted the embryonic principle contained in the Places of Worship (Enfranchisement) Act 1920: 'a house which a tenant has leased for more than twenty-one years shall be taken to belong to him and not to the ground landlord.' Crossman supported him and the principle, but proceeded to knock him down at Cabinet by pointing out that if the Bill applied to public property it was not socialist, but if it did not it would be 'impossible to defend'.[43]

Further tensions developed. When it was suggested that a clause requiring leaseholders to have owned the lease for twenty-one years be included, Crossman replied that if this were accepted 'there would be an appalling shemozzle in South

---

41 Crossman (17 Nov. 1964) in Crossman (1975) p. 59.
42 Crossman (23 Dec. 1965) in ibid. p. 420.
43 Crossman (19 Oct. 1965) in ibid. p. 353; Crossman (23 Dec. 1965) in ibid. p. 420.

Wales and Birmingham' even though 'of course, morality is on the side of the lawyers. If we are concerned with morality we should certainly introduce a 21-year limitation.'[44] In the end he got his way but the lawyers resisted drafting the Bill, which led to legal trouble later on. Still, the Bill now existed – although it would have to wait, as Wilson called another election. After the Labour Party won that election, Crossman became Leader of the House of Commons, and so was mainly concerned with getting leasehold reform on the statute book.

The Bill's passage through Parliament put all these problems into the shade. Despite copious criticism by the opposition (focused not on the principle of enfranchisement but on how much the tenant would benefit compared to the landlord), the Bill was never really in jeopardy – the popular pressure for it was too strong. The danger was that the government would lose control of it. The biggest fight was about which properties the Bill would apply to. As originally proposed, all houses under a certain rateable value (£400 in London and £200 outside) on leases of twenty-one years or more were judged to belong to the lessee (subject to a few modest qualifications such as length of residence), with the lessor owning only the land. The lessee was empowered to buy out the landlord at any point, or to get a new 50-year lease at the end of their current lease on those terms. Of course 'those terms' made little economic sense, and so the prices paid were subject to arbitration.

MPs who wanted the Bill to go further seized on the rateable value limit. Why, they argued, did a principle of justice stop when a house became marginally more valuable? Why was the magic figure £200? (The answer was that this was the figure used

---

44 Crossman (10 Feb. 1966) in Crossman (1975) p. 452.

The Avalanche

in the Rent Act 1965, but it was not a very persuasive one.)[45] A story was unearthed by Evan Luard, Oxford's Labour MP, of a tenant who had made improvements to his house at his own expense and in consequence was lifted just over the threshold.[46] Luard had been a Research Fellow at St Anthony's but felt no compulsion to help another college: he explicitly noted that the limits would exclude 250 houses owned by St John's and supported an amendment to raise the rateable value limit in Oxford and Cambridge.[47] The problem was that the legislation was a giveaway to tenants, and so including more valuable houses could see massive windfalls going to the very rich, which did not seem like good socialist praxis. Similarly the exclusion of local authorities made little sense in terms of justice, but a lot in terms of ideology.

Unpersuaded by the theorists, the MPs amended the Bill in the Committee Stage, voting 18 to 1 to remove the rateable value limits. The Cabinet ordered the change removed; a flurry of amendments to remove the removal of the removal of the limits followed. Parliament was treated to the spectacle of supportive Labour MPs claiming that the government was not giving its real reasons to the House and alleging a conspiracy with the Church Commissioners and the aristocracy – all the more unedifying because both claims were true.[48] The government got its way, but at the cost of laying bare the Bill's shoddy justification. On top of all this, the Bill was badly drafted. Further legislation had to be passed in 1969 to deal with an issue where unclear wording

---

45 *Hansard*. HC Deb. Vol. 748 Col. 1491 (20 June 1967).
46 Ibid. Col. 1502 (20 June 1967).
47 Ibid. Cols. 1501–2 (20 June 1967).
48 Ibid. Cols. 1495–6, 1505, 1514 (20 June 1967). For lobbying by the Church Commissioners and aristocracy see Chapter 5.

had resulted in prices for enfranchising tenants being set higher than the government had intended – something the Bill's original critics delighted in pointing out they had criticised (albeit in a rather general manner) all along.[49]

The Parliamentary debate revealed just how populist the Bill was, but this had been predictable. In 1961 George Thomas, a Welsh Labour MP, had led a debate calling for the government to introduce leasehold reform in Wales. The debate saw Labour MPs calling for houses to be essentially given away at the end of the lease – suggesting that the formulation Labour adopted when drafting the 1967 Act was not so much a breakthrough as an acceptance of the base's demands – and Callaghan reiterating that leasehold enfranchisement had been Labour policy since 1951.[50] Tensions ran high: implicitly contrasting his constituents with the Welsh, Conservative MP Henry Brooke (Minister for Welsh Affairs) said he had had no issues with leaseholds because 'remarkably few people in Hampstead are so gullible or stupid as to imagine that they have acquired the freehold interest when they have actually acquired the leasehold'.[51]

The reaction to Conservative MP John Foster, who identified himself as a director of Western Ground Rents, was even more fierce. Since buying the Butes' Cardiff property, the company had become notorious in Wales for engaging in unreasonable behaviour and not allowing tenants to buy their homes except at what were considered excessive prices. Foster's intervention in defence of the company was variously labelled as 'extraordinary … deplorable … reprehensible … a breach of privilege … utterly

---

49 *Hansard.* HC Deb. Vol. 784 Col. 744 (22 May 1969).
50 *Hansard.* HC Deb. Vol. 644 Cols. 456–7 (12 July 1961).
51 *Hansard.* HC Deb. Vol. 644 Col. 461 (12 July 1961).

disgraceful ... a disgusting exhibition ... in shocking taste'.[52] His extended defence of his employer was indeed in poor taste, but it consisted of a point-by-point refutation of the claims made by George Thomas, both in the House and in newspapers. These refutations were challenged but not themselves refuted: Thomas does seem to have been careless with the facts. But this should not surprise us. Leasehold reform had two aspects: a positive-sum question about how tenure could be reformed so that it worked best for society; and a zero-sum question about how the assets being reformed would be divided up. Failures to deal with the former question had understandably exacerbated tensions; the resulting legislation – badly drafted, justified on grounds no one believed, and in Crossman's words not 'redistribut[ing] income according to social need because its application is completely arbitrary' – was the expression of this frustration combined with political ambition.[53]

This assessment is borne out by the Act's political aftermath. It was unsurprising that a Labour MP for Oxford would not be sympathetic to the interests of a landowning college; more interestingly Montague Woodhouse, Oxford's Conservative MP, who lost his seat to Luard in 1966 and regained it in 1970, also came round to supporting reform. This was despite personal lobbying from the Duke of Westminster, whose own properties were affected by the change.[54] Woodhouse was a remarkable man who had spent the Second World War behind enemy lines blowing up bridges and organising resistance in Greece. He also had experience representing unhappy leaseholders to the College.[55] But although he

---

52 *Hansard*. HC Deb. Vol. 644 Cols. 428–9, 434 (12 July 1961).
53 Crossman (21 Feb. 1967) in Crossman (1976) p. 248.
54 Personal correspondence.
55 SJC ADM II.C.3 (27 Oct. 1960).

may have been readier to come to his own opinions than most, he was not alone. Hugh Rossi, another Conservative MP, criticised the Bill throughout its Parliamentary passage; but in 1974 he was successfully pushing for it to be extended to even more dwellings. Following this he worked on the policy that would become Margaret Thatcher's Right to Buy: after all, if it was right that tenants could enfranchise themselves against private landlords, was it not also right that they could enfranchise themselves against the state? Of course Labour saw things differently – but Rossi had realised that these policies were vote winners, and it had already been established that an exemption for the state was not really defensible. Labour was weakened by the old debate over whether the right policy was state ownership or egalitarian household ownership. The Conservatives had no such hang-ups: a property-owning democracy was clearly in their interests, and if it was sweetened with giveaways, so much the better. Taking the long view, Labour's hasty reform looks like a stunning political own goal.

What Could St John's Have Done?

What would a historically minded investor have observed in the run-up to 1967? Since the 1890s there had been pressure for leasehold enfranchisement and attempts in Parliament to achieve it. These had gone nowhere and the issue had lost some of its relevance after the First World War, but it had shown an interesting tendency to attract politicians across the spectrum, many of whom focused on the benefits it would bring to current lessees rather than on the fundamental issues with the legal form of tenure. A series of measures to deal with the problem had been brought in but none had been very successful. Since the 1950s, Labour Party policy had been to deliver leasehold enfranchisement. Debating positions, meanwhile, were becoming

The Avalanche

increasingly extreme on both sides, while in the background a large number of leases were coming very close to falling in. Given all this, what could reasonably be expected of the College's investment policy?

We can picture a continuum on which a reasonable expectation of the Fellowship's knowledge could be placed. At one end is complete ignorance: imagine the College's property holdings were not on its doorstep but in Japan, administered by an investment trust, and no Fellow had any knowledge of the country. At the other end would be something like complete certainty: a tip-off from a friendly Cabinet minister with oversight of the reform. We would not expect the appropriate investment decision to be a linear function of this knowledge, since even a fairly detailed awareness of the political threat might not put the College ahead of other sophisticated investors and thus the risk might be appropriately priced. Given the specific constraints around selling residential property, however, the level of knowledge held by other relevant investors might have been quite low. Furthermore, even if the College was completely ignorant of the political risk its investments were exposed to, the argument for diversification set out by Richardson would have held good. Set against this, we must remember that the College had plans to redevelop part of the estate and use the rest to finance the development: these complicated the decision regarding diversification but would have been less attractive the greater the short-term risk the College felt the investment was exposed to.

Our question therefore has two sides. The first is whether St John's could and should have anticipated that its long leases in North Oxford were especially risky, which would have strengthened the argument for diversifying beyond the standard reasons for doing so. The second is whether the College chose to gamble that the value of leaseholds would not fall, and whether such a bet was sensible, both on its face and given the actions of other market participants.

What did the Fellowship know? In 1959 Richardson had written his memo noting how concentrated their endowment was in North Oxford. This did not explicitly refer to the risk of leasehold enfranchisement, but it should have prompted the Fellows to give the matter more thought than they might have normally done. It is too much to expect them to trace the history of protest for leasehold enfranchisement back to the 1890s, and even if they had it did not necessarily suggest that reform would be confiscatory. But there were things they should have been aware of: current Labour Party policy, for example. They did not lack warnings: the 1960 Report on the Future of the North Oxford Estate prepared by Cluttons had explicitly warned about the dangers of leasehold enfranchisement.[56] St John's had sent that report to Lord Harcourt and had taken the warning seriously enough to include it in an accompanying letter: 'Of this residential property, some 1,500 houses are outstanding on ground lease and would thus be exposed to any future legislation permitting leasehold enfranchisement.'[57] It was the arguments against the proposal to divest from North Oxford by Lord Harcourt and others which persuaded the College to change course and plan to redevelop Walton Manor.

Given this, it is hard to see the Fellowship's action as anything other than burying its head in the sand. On the continuum laid out above, they should have been closer to full knowledge than ignorance: the threat was not obscure and advisors explicitly warned them about it. Even the most casual analysis of the situation would suggest that their investments were at risk – they

---

56 SJC EST I.E.16 (Mar. 1969).
57 SJC MUN V.C.64 (June 1960) p. 1.

knew they were an unpopular landlord and they knew leasehold was increasingly unacceptable as a form of tenure – and that it would almost certainly spell doom for their redevelopment plans in Walton Manor. It is true that divesting from their North Oxford property was not as simple as it could have been – but we will see in Chapter 5 that they could plausibly have offloaded a lot of it. In any case, they had already decided to do so in 1960 before they changed their minds.

The situation is better understood as a clash of narratives. As discussed in Chapter 2, the bursar was attracted to the idea of St John's being a benevolent 'lord of the manor'; many of the Fellows appear to have felt the same, or at least to have given undue attention to the interests of the Oxford Preservation Trust relative to the College's financial wellbeing. In theory nothing prevented them from holding this view while recognising threats from political change. But in practice we struggle to hold multiple contradictory narratives in our mind at once. The idea that angry tenants might drive an ascendent Labour Party to empower them to enfranchise themselves – perhaps at a confiscatory rate – against the benevolent College would have resulted in cognitive dissonance.

The financial theory was clear: high concentrations of value in one type of asset are risky at the best of times. They are even more risky when the asset is at risk of becoming a binary bet: either enfranchisement would happen or it wouldn't. And they became riskier still when the effective value of the assets had been increased because the College was basing its future financial plans on redeveloping them. There really was no excuse for seeing the warning signs, deciding to take action by divesting, and then changing plans to double down on the exposed assets. But the trouble goes deeper than that.

Even if the Fellows had not been following the situation

closely – and they should have been – the populist anger with respect to leaseholds and the increasingly raucous displays in Parliament should have challenged their narrative that all was well among the tenants. It should have prompted them to reflect on the many social and political changes that had occurred since the 1850s and question whether leasehold really was acceptable in their time. It is too much to say that anyone could have seen that leasehold reform would occur in 1967, for houses rated at or below £200, with a price based on the freeholder owning only the land. But the Fellowship *could* have seen that leasehold reform was likely to occur sooner or later; that the area it wanted to redevelop was not expensive enough that it was likely to escape the net; and that when reform came it was likely to be with a level of compensation for landlords that would devastate their endowment. They were responsible.

4

A LITTLE LEARNING

Why Did St John's Become Academically Successful?

The clever men at Oxford
Know all that there is to be knowed.
      Kenneth Grahame, *The Wind in the Willows*, 1908

After reform in the 1860s, the teaching at St John's was so bad that a student like Charles Yates Fell could mourn his disappointing exam results without seeing how things could have turned out differently. The 1890s saw a dedicated Senior Tutor trying to improve the College and being thanked with the loss of his Fellowship. Standards at Oxford improved after the Second World War as access became less exclusive, but this applied to all the colleges: St John's was still an academic backwater. And then – or so the story recited at High Table goes – everything changed under the leadership of President Southern. Suddenly the College went from nowhere to the top of the Norrington Table, its Fellowship contained some of the best academics in Oxford, and it never looked back. Is this really what happened?

 Academic success can be easy to sense but hard to quantify. Colleges do many things: teaching undergraduates; supporting graduate students; and providing an atmosphere for academic

Intellectual Capital

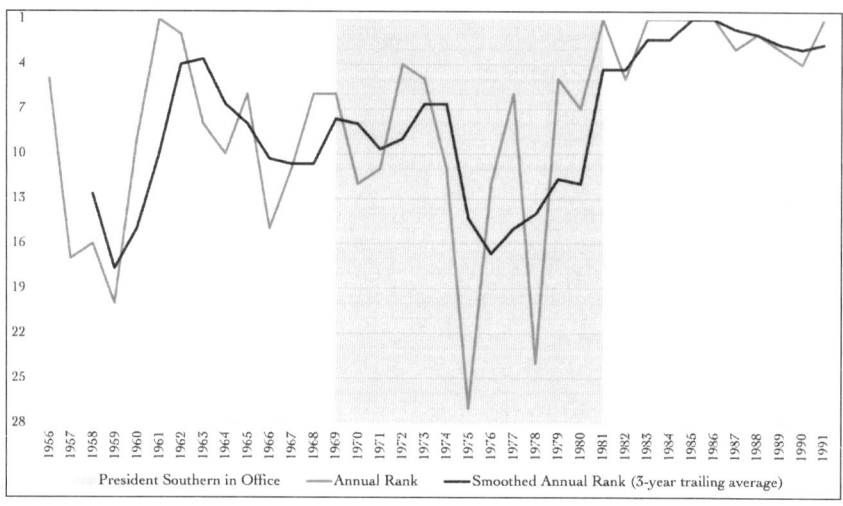

Figure 4.1: The College's Norrington Table Ranking

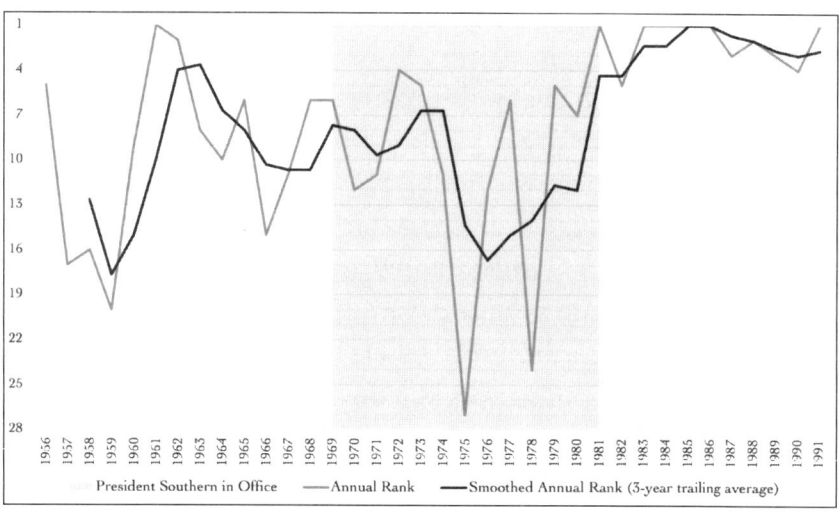

Figure 4.2: Members of the Fellowship who would become Fellows of the British Academy or Royal Society

research. We do not even have the luxury of saying, for example, that better exam results are evidence of greater success: what if they were achieved by driving students to focus on work at the expense of sports and cultural activities, such as stabbing each other in the back at the Union? On the other hand, we can surely say *something* about a college's academic precession or regression. So what data do we have?

Figures 4.1 and 4.2 (already seen in Chapter 1) reveal some aspects of the picture that are susceptible to quantification. The Norrington Table is a ranking of colleges based on their undergraduates' performances in their Final Honour Schools. We can see that results were volatile but generally middling in the 1950s and 60s; they improved somewhat in the early 1970s but then took a turn for the worse, before shooting up in 1979 and staying at the top throughout the 1980s. From this, it would seem that change began to occur in the late 1970s – or perhaps two or three years earlier than that, as presumably the undergraduates did not wake up one day in 1979 and spontaneously decide to excel.

Another perspective is gained by looking at the Fellowship. Performance here is harder to judge than for the undergraduates, but we can use the proportion of Fellows who were, or would become, Fellows of the British Academy or Royal Society as a proxy. This is certainly an imperfect measure of achievement but it is one we would expect to be correlated with underlying ability, and represents a judgement by academics' peers about the quality of their work. Here we see steady improvement from around 1900 to 1950; thereafter the proportion slightly declines, although the absolute number of Fellows continues to increase. This is explained by the Fellowship itself dramatically increasing in size, but it does suggest that this was not at the expense of ability. Still, the picture we get is of an SCR that peaked in the 1950s but broadly remained at that level thereafter.

The academic destinations of Fellows of St John's is another proxy for ability, but this is inherently much more subjective, especially as Fellows found their way into a whole variety of roles across the world. The proportion going on to significant chairs or gaining titles of distinction at Oxford does increase over time, and especially sharply in the late 1960s and late 1980s, but this is partially because more opportunities were being created. It is therefore hard to infer very much from it, except to note that it is consistent with an increasingly successful Fellowship.

The first thing this tells us is that there is not going to be a simple story. Different parts of St John's seem to have improved at different points. However, there is one important commonality between all these measures: they all improved over time, and by 1980 they were all as good, or almost as good, as they ever had been. So there was progress. What caused it?

The most common theory is that President Southern, assisted by the dons he led and inspired, transformed St John's from an academic backwater into a powerhouse. There is a lot to be said for this argument – not least the fact that many people who experienced Southern's rule believe it to be true. Southern became President in 1969 and retired in 1981, which does overlap with some – but not all – of the period of quantifiable improvement. A second theory is that it was thanks to the College's wealth – both the absolute wealth, and the fact that much of it was involuntarily made available owing to leasehold enfranchisement and the Fellows had to decide what to do with it – that St John's could improve its teaching and attract better students and Fellows. Finally there is a third theory, advocated half jokingly by Keith Thomas, that it was down to luck. A grain of good fortune, accidentally swallowed by an oyster-like College, could have catalysed a response which grew until, almost before anyone realised it, something valuable had been created. And of course there is no reason to believe that these theories are mutually exclusive.

Change Comes from the Top

Was it all the work of President Southern? We should take seriously the belief of those at the time who thought it was – much of the richness of the past is lost to the historian, and we all are confident of many things in our daily lives for which we might struggle to muster documentary or physical evidence. Even apart from this, there is much to support the theory. Southern was determined to improve the College's academic standing: upon arrival he gathered all the second- and third-year undergraduates in Hall and then, walking up and down and gesturing at the portraits hanging there, upbraided the students for the College's performance. They had a fantastic library, excellent resources, all the potential in the world: there was no reason for them to achieve second-rate results.[1]

Certainly this was part of Southern's reason for coming to the College. As we saw in Chapter 1, it was not a decision he made lightly or immediately. As the Chichele Professor of History at All Souls, he was at the very peak of his academic powers: prestigious as running a college could be, in research terms it was a serious downgrade. Hugh Trevor-Roper did not only express his bemusement at Southern's decision pseudonymously; in a letter to Valerie Pearl on 4 April 1969 he wrote, 'The great problem in Oxford is the Chichele Chair, vacated by Dick Southern, who prefers the Presidency of St John's (an odd preference).'[2] And Southern had turned down college headships before. But St John's gave him

---

1 Private conversation.
2 Trevor-Roper (2014) p. 186.

the opportunity to focus on improving teaching, which he had been wanting to do anyway. All Souls famously consisted only of Fellows, and the 1966 Franks Report on the University had criticised it sharply for 'infirmity of purpose'. It had considered taking graduate students by merging with St Anthony's, but the plan had come to nothing and it was decided to create a class of Visiting Fellows instead.[3] The faction that had wanted graduates at All Souls included Southern and Isaiah Berlin, who left to become the founding President of Wolfson College in 1966. St John's, with its expansion plans, offered an opportunity for Southern to realise this aim. He was so assiduous in achieving it that he offended some members of the SCR who felt he was more available to the students than he was to them.

Southern did not limit himself to exhortation but was active in reforming St John's. There were minor changes – Collections, which traditionally take place at the end of term and where each student's performance is described by their tutors to the President, were changed to feature written reports, so he could have a better overview of how each student was doing and where help might be needed – and major ones – more Tutorial Fellows were hired to improve teaching for undergraduates, their numbers jumping from sixteen to twenty-six in 1971 alone.[4] We have seen that this hiring spree was not at the expense of ability; remarkably gifted people found their way to St John's. They were also increasingly unlikely to have been at St John's – or even at Oxford – as students, suggesting that the College was more open to talent wherever it could find it. Interestingly, one thing that did not markedly change was the age or average tenure of the members of Governing Body – one might have expected it

---

3 Lowe (1998) pp. 201–4.
4 SJC ADM IV.A.3.b.

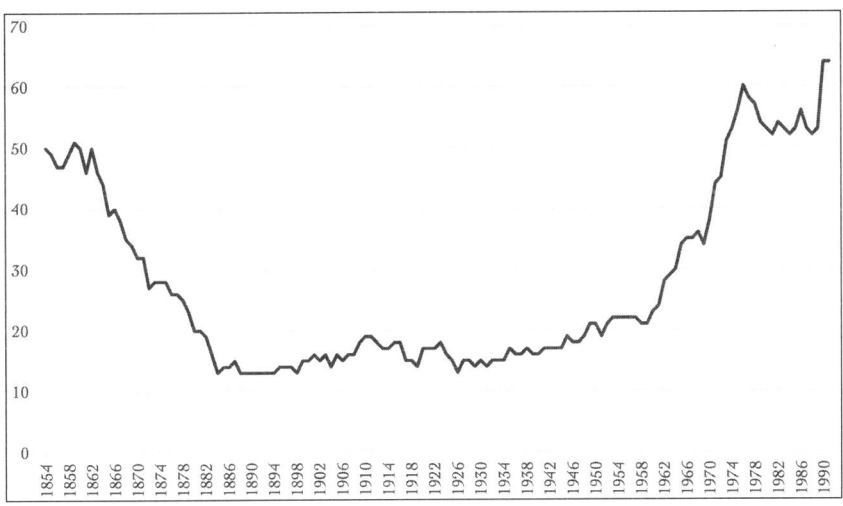

Figure 4.3: Number of Fellows

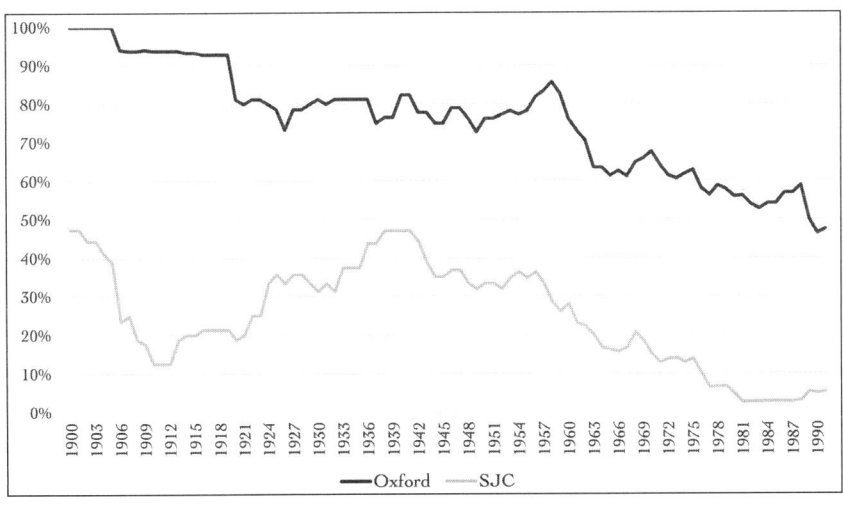

Figure 4.4: Academic Origins of Members of Governing Body

Intellectual Capital

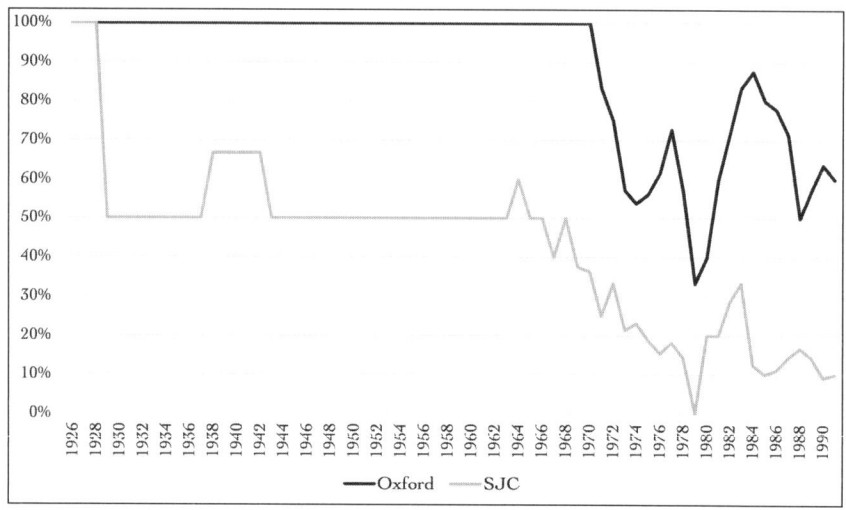

Figure 4.5: Academic Origins of Junior Research Fellows

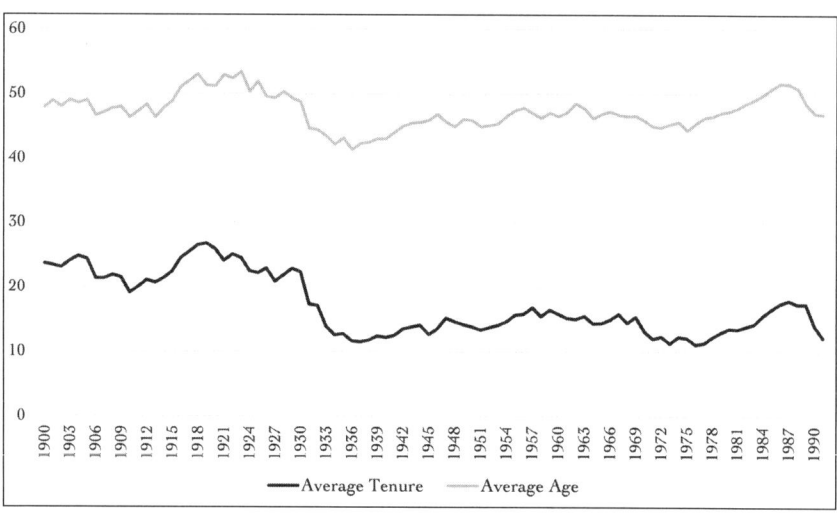

Figure 4.6: Average Age and Tenure of Members of Governing Body

to get younger and fresher, but a similar balance of vitality and experience seems to have been maintained.

Contrasting the change at St John's with the changes at University College highlights another aspect of Southern's role. As Figure 4.7 shows, University College saw a similar relative improvement in its Norrington scores a few years before St John's did. In part, the reason was a change driven by two dons: Leslie Mitchell and in particular John Albery, who from 1968 was Tutor for Admissions. Frustrated at the standard of undergraduate admissions – they found the College was filled with lovely chaps who might be good at sport but weren't always that academic – Albery centralised the admissions procedure by making it a competition.[5] As well as having its core allocated spaces, each subject could now compete for additional spaces – but this involved making your case to all the other tutors at admissions meetings that ran late into the night. The process forced everyone to have defensible reasons for wanting extra candidates; and the only defensible reason was that 'they're better than the one you're proposing'. Admissions standards, and then results, duly improved.

Albery also proved to be a highly diligent Tutor for Admissions: he was legendary for using the exhibitions and scholarships the college could offer to poach good candidates from other colleges. All his changes meant that even if the teaching hadn't improved, University College had more promising men to work with. But the teaching did get better as well: the whole atmosphere of the college changed and became more focused on ensuring its students achieved academic success. Fellows worried about their Norrington rank and would brag to each other over lunch about how many of their students had got Firsts.

---

5 Interview with Leslie Mitchell.

Intellectual Capital

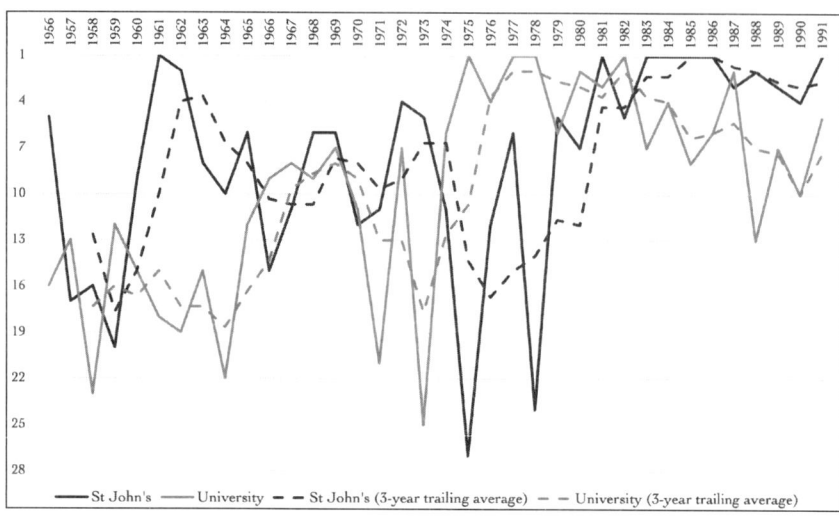

Figure 4.7: Comparison of St John's and University College's ranking in the Norrington Table

The situation at St John's was, in some ways, quite similar. As early as the 1950s and 60s the College had some very good academics who excelled at teaching: for example Harold Thompson, Keith Thomas, and John Carey. But while they wanted good students, this was only in their subject area – or at least, that was where they had influence. Unlike University College, St John's did not have a central committee which forced all the dons to compete. This was one area where Southern, determined to drive up standards across the College, doubtless made a significant difference. It is also interesting to note that it was some years after the appointment of both Albery and Southern that exam results began to improve in their colleges. Even accounting for the three-year lag for any change in admissions policy to feed through into results, this shows that it took time for the changes to have their full effect.

Despite all this, there are reasons to question how much of the improvement at St John's can be personally attributed to Southern. The most obvious point is that the signs of improvement in the data do not neatly line up with his arrival, even accounting for a three-year lag in Norrington Table results. Relative exam performance actually dipped for a few years before it began to be consistently strong from 1979. This is certainly compatible with the College taking time to change, but it is not as neat a correlation as we might have expected it to be. As for the Fellowship, there is no obvious sign of change, except that it became much larger – and it was already growing. In any case, Southern did not have personal discretion as to who was hired.

An even more important point is that Southern was not thrust upon St John's but was elected by the Fellowship. Since 1948, St John's had elected its most or second most senior Fellow to the Presidency, but in 1969 there was no appetite to do so. Many serious external candidates were put forward, and the internal ones, too, were respected academics. It is possible that Keith Thomas, who clearly worked to persuade the Fellowship to elect Southern and prepared a summary of his academic and administrative experience for them, had spoken to him privately about the opportunity – but as we know Southern was unsure about the job even when he was formally offered it, so it seems unlikely that he was exerting pressure on the College. It really does seem to have been a case of the dons deciding that they wanted change, and a suitable person to lead them in it. This has two important implications: the change did not start with Southern; and when he arrived he found a College full of people who supported his plans.

If both Southern and the dons played an important role in changing St John's, how can we determine their relative contributions? Again the contrast with University College is instructive. There the Masters (University College's heads of house) played little role beyond not getting in the way; but general change still needed a central figure supported by a group of dons. St John's seems to have decided to use the Presidency for this role, and it seems likely that whoever was appointed would have tried to perform it. But Southern was clearly exceptional: he gave all his energy to the job but, crucially, all his thought as well. Another President, however well-intentioned, might not have done so.

One way to understand the change in academic outcomes is through a simple input–output model. If St John's hired more tutors, provided more facilities, and increased tutors' engagement by encouraging and exhorting them more, then academic outcomes would improve as students were enabled to do better (and, noticing this, better students would choose to come to the College in the first place). An alternative model focuses on the College as an academic community. A few hundred students and Fellows, all living on top of one another in medieval buildings, eating in the same Hall, and praying in the same chapel, will be influenced by each other in ways that go beyond the number of hours they spend in tutorials. Everyone will be affected – not necessarily decisively, but significantly – by everyone else. If your tutor expects you to work for a First and your peers are doing so, that becomes the path of least resistance (unless other temptations, such as spending the evening at the Lamb & Flag rather than writing another essay, come into play). Contrast this with John Carey's experience: 'my conversations with a number of other freshmen assured me that they were not among the masterminds of the western world. How one or two of them got into Oxford at all puzzled me.'[6] Something changed, and that change was self-perpetuating: at least one chemist remembers that 'the true myth that St John's was THE place to apply to

---

6 Carey (2015) p. 95.

if you were a chemist self-promulgated', and this was certainly true for other disciplines too.[7] From this perspective, Southern's crucial role may have been in providing a shock to the system, allowing the College to move from one state of equilibrium to another.

An equilibrium model explains why St John's continued to do so well academically after Southern retired and John Kendrew was elected. Kendrew had won a Nobel Prize in Chemistry for his work on proteins and was, by all accounts, a lovely man who thought deeply about College business (and left St John's a generous legacy). But he was rarely seen around the College.[8] When his portrait was unveiled in the Hall, Fellows joked that now the undergraduates could see who their President had been. His tenure was nevertheless marked by even greater Norrington success than Southern's had been. This was perhaps Southern's biggest achievement: both in terms of academic results and the kind of person the Fellowship turned to for leadership, success had become institutionalised at St John's.

Success isn't Given, it's Bought

The Leasehold Reform Act 1967 was a disaster for the College's endowment, but it did mean that a lot of money was suddenly released for use. One option would have been to put this back into the endowment by buying more equities. Newly freed, however, from the Ministry of Agriculture's control, the Fellows of St John's began to contemplate something more radical: new accommodation which would enable St John's to house all its

---

[7] Correspondence with Steve Postle (m. 1969). Other alumni mentioned that St John's had a similar reputation in other areas, such as History.
[8] Wassarman (2020) p. 226.

undergraduates throughout their entire degree. Such provision would be almost unique in the University and might help the College to attract better applicants, as well as strengthening its community. And it would be an opportunity to gain other amenities like an underground car park and a swimming pool. Of course this was just one way the money could be used: new tutorial Fellowships could be created, or more research Fellows hired.

One thing that was not done was to give more to students directly. After accounting for inflation, spending on scholarships and similar transfers fluctuated but did not display a meaningful trend from 1967 to 1981. In contrast, real spending on tuition rose 124 per cent throughout Southern's tenure (although undergraduate numbers also rose 34 per cent). The College additionally spent £1.5m building the Sir Thomas White Building (although as noted in Chapter 1 they did not intend to spend that much, and the swimming pool and underground car park fell by the wayside). The opportunity this offered for all undergraduates to spend their entire degrees living in the College was rare at the time. The comparison with University College's Stavertonia is again interesting: it was completed in 1974, a year before the Sir Thomas White Building, and was used 'ruthlessly' in admissions to persuade applicants of the virtues of applying to the college.[9]

How important were the new buildings? Eyeballing the Norrington results suggests that University College's academic ascent had begun before any benefit from applications had had time to filter through, but the offer of full accommodation can't have hurt the situation. The year 1978, the first in which applicants to St John's who might have been swayed by the new building sat their Finals, was the second-worst on record – but 1979 was much better, and thereafter the College began to dominate the

---

9 Interview with Leslie Mitchell.

Norrington Table. Certainly several alumni remember the offer of full accommodation being an attraction. But the building was not just a carrot to lure applicants: Geoffrey Tyack notes that 'with the relocation of the Junior Common Room [to the new building] the college's centre of gravity shifted towards the north.'[10] Having more students closer together helped strengthen the community, providing a happier and more supportive atmosphere which is likely to have fed through to better exam results – especially given that it was often the Finalists who had had to live out in rented accommodation.

So how important was the money? It is difficult to see how the College could have expanded – both in terms of Tutorial Fellows and the Sir Thomas White building – without it. And without the means to afford these developments, it is quite possible that President Southern would not have wanted the job, had he been offered it. The College's wealth, then, played a crucial role. But it seems unlikely that wealth was the driving factor in the College's improvement. The money could have been spent on many other things: the endowment; hiring even more new research Fellows; even on better facilities for the dons. It was very easy for a rich college to spend its money unwisely – the Epilogue describes how Magdalen College did just that. Instead St John's poured the money into expanding accommodation for students and improving their learning experience. That was not inevitable.

The Gifts of Tyche

Polybius argued that, when other causal explanations have been exhausted, we can attribute the reasons for an event to the whim

---

10 Tyack (2005) p. 79.

of Tyche, the goddess of fortune.[11] Modern statistics has taken the opposite route: the starting assumption is that everything is due to luck, and we need good evidence to believe otherwise. History sits somewhere in between, recognising that both approaches have something to offer. In consideration of Polybius' historical precedence, we will consider the more qualitative aspects of luck in the College's story before turning to a regression analysis.

Luck plays two explanatory roles. The first is as an adjunct to other models of change: for example, it is very easy to imagine Southern choosing not to take the Presidency when it was offered to him, but it is harder to imagine the Fellows not electing someone of high academic distinction. The more weight we put on Southern's personal role, the more important luck is in the story; the more weight we put on the Fellows' role and see the election of Southern as a signal of their intent, the less important luck is.

The second is as a model in its own right. If a college is susceptible to feedback loops – perhaps because it has the potential for multiple equilibria of the sort discussed above – then random variations can have disproportionate effects over time. Hiring one good tutor can give a college a better reputation for teaching; that tutor could push for similar tutors to themselves and influence the selection of future undergraduates.

It is clear that the first sort of luck is important. It was lucky that the College, acting on instructions from its Founder, owned land that became immensely valuable. It was lucky that some Fellows of immense ability joined: Keith Thomas, for example, arrived in 1957 after his Fellowship at All Souls mainly because the job was available; St John's didn't seem anything special to

---

11 Polybius (1979) pp. 537–9.

him at the time. It was lucky that Southern was willing to take the Presidency. Luck in this sense does not explain anything, but it is a helpful reminder that things might easily have been different.

The second sort of luck, however, offers an explanatory framework. What if it was just an initial grain of good luck – perhaps happening to hire an exceptional tutor – which led to better students, more energised dons, better hiring practices, a majority for a reforming President? One reason to doubt this story is that the initial kind of change posited was happening all over Oxford, albeit in different ways. The massive expansion in university access after the Second World War had resulted in the presence of a much wider class of young academics, many of whom wanted to reform practices which appeared ridiculous. John Carey was one example – an exceptional tutor at St John's, he had already been an exceptional tutor at Keble. We saw above how the College began to take more and more men from outside its walls and even from beyond Oxford: there was too much talent available not to do so. St John's was drawing from an enlarged and improved urn: different draws would certainly have changed the colour, but not the general shape, of its story.

Change in the Wider University

General change beyond the College explains why two other factors, both extremely important, are nonetheless not satisfying candidates for its relative improvement. The first is the admission of women. Until 1974, women studying at Oxford were confined to women's colleges, but there had been growing pressure to change the situation. The University, worried about change in general but also about the risk to the women's colleges, decided to trial co-education, and allowed five colleges to accept a mixed intake.[12] The plan was to carefully study the outcomes. In the event, no study was needed. In 1979 the University was confronted with many colleges wanting to admit women. It attempted to impose order by running a lottery to establish which five colleges could become mixed next, but University College announced that it was going to do so whether it won the lottery or not. Hearing this, St John's decided to adopt the same stance. Other colleges subsequently followed their lead, and in 1979 almost all the colleges became mixed.

Admitting women clearly helped a college's academic performance simply by increasing the pool of qualified applicants. But it also had an effect on the general character of the place. Tim Connolly (m. 1978) remembers how 'this change made St John's a much more natural social entity … personally I believe that social cohesion breeds a positive and supportive atmosphere whatever the endeavour – which in St John's case was getting a good degree.' Although it was hard to pinpoint the exact reasons why it improved the College's academic performance, 'I feel sure that it did.'[13] For this reason and many others, the admission of women is a very important part of the College's history.

Following University College in threatening to defy the University's edict on the number of colleges which could admit women was certainly a sign that St John's was serious about academic achievement (and possibly gender equality). In the event, however, the other colleges adopted the same stance, so the benefits of admitting women accrued to all of them (apart from Christ Church, which waited a year, and Oriel, which waited six). The women's colleges were unfortunately hurt by the change – no longer able to take the cream of their own

---

12 These were Jesus, Wadham, Hertford, Brasenose, and St Catherine's.
13 Private correspondence.

application pool, they found themselves in competition with older, richer colleges – and their relative decline provided a boost to all the other colleges. It is also possible that having a larger applicant pool reinforced the position of more selective colleges, which St John's had become, by making the benefits of being able to choose who you selected greater.[14] Nevertheless, admitting women was not a change that was unique to St John's and so it does not explain why the College improved so much relative to most of the others.

Another factor that was extremely important, but not unique to St John's, was a general change in admissions throughout the University. After the Second World War, access had increased dramatically, but the University was still dominated by boys from public and private schools. This began to change as more tutors came from different backgrounds and were determined to offer young people the same opportunities they had received; there was also a growing realisation that there was a lot of talent in the grammar schools (and beyond) and that an ambitious college, if it cultivated links with schools, could secure a good supply of exceptional applicants.

St John's was certainly selective, with tutors determined to find the best candidates – recall John Carey's horror in Chapter 1 that Keble was admitting students based on rowing, rather than academic, ability. Applicants were also aware of St John's reputation from at least the late 1970s, and it would have encouraged schools to recommend stronger candidates to the College.

---

14 One way to test this is to look at the volatility of Norrington Table results: by how much did a college's rank change, on average, from one year to the next? The volatility does decline from 1982, in line with this theory, but not very much, and so many other changes were occurring at the time which are plausibly correlated with the decision to admit women that we cannot isolate the effect.

But St John's was not alone in its approach, and in fact not even at the forefront of the change. That honour probably goes to Hertford College, where the Tutor for Admissions, Neil Tanner, set up what became known as the 'Tanner Scheme' to encourage applications from schools which did not traditionally send students to Oxford. Lawrence Goldman's history of the scheme noted that other colleges also participated in regional schemes – for example, a few colleges reserved two places annually for students from schools in West Yorkshire, based on the recommendation of their headmasters and interviews – but they were unpopular with other colleges, although (or perhaps because) they were very successful.[15] The Tanner Scheme aimed to deal with a more general problem: applicants to Oxford usually had to spend a seventh term in the sixth form studying for entrance exams, which was prohibitively expensive for many students. Therefore they simply didn't apply.

Tanner's solution was to create an extra pathway to admission. Early in the second year of sixth form – the time most applicants apply today – headmasters would recommend students and they would be given interviews at Hertford. Those who impressed would receive offers with no requirements (apart from the very minimal ones the University required for matriculation). To build links with those headmasters, school visits by dons were encouraged; as Tanner noted, 'If we wait for the schools to appreciate our sterling qualities, we shall be taking Balliol rejects one hundred years from now.'[16] The scheme was immensely successful and was credited with turning Hertford's Norrington Table performance around: it went from being in the mid-twenties in the 1960s and 70s to regularly being in the

---

15 Goldman (2018) pp. 8–11.
16 Tanner quoted in ibid. p. 20.

top ten in the 1980s. In the 1980s Tanner noted that the proportion of students getting Firsts at Oxford during the duration of the scheme was 12 per cent, whereas 33 per cent of students who came to Hertford under it achieved Firsts. Applications to Hertford also soared.[17] Other colleges – but not St John's – began to copy the scheme in the 1980s, and the University, again worried about chaos, established a new admissions procedure for all the colleges which took on some of the ideas in the Tanner Scheme.[18]

Just as in many other colleges, the impetus for the Tanner Scheme came from concerns among younger dons that Hertford was not doing as well academically as it could – they pointed to its Norrington Table results as evidence – and that part of the problem was an over-reliance on independent schools. Such schools were adept at getting borderline cases into colleges, which could decrease the academic quality of the student body. This had always gone on, especially in the days when college heads of house were more influential in admissions or when some other famous friend could be used to lobby for entry. In the contentious election for the University Chancellorship in 1960, Hugh Trevor-Roper canvassed support by writing 'to every parent whose son I had ever jobbed into Christ Church'. One, acknowledging that Trevor-Roper 'put my candidate in', duly showed up with a crate of champagne; a baronet was persuaded to break his journey from Paris to the Cheltenham races at the polling booth. (Trevor-Roper was already unimpressed with St John's, which 'remained sunk in grubby neutrality'

---

17 Goldman (2018) pp. 29, 33.
18 Although St John's may have considered it, as the President went to a lunch at Hertford to work out how the scheme operated (Goldman, 2018, p. 48).

during the contest.)¹⁹ But it remained true: in his diaries John Rae, the headmaster of Westminster, recalls a deal he struck whereby Christ Church would take 'the odd borderline case' (albeit to secure some better candidates as well). On other occasions he noted how applicants could be awarded a place with a few (or many) phone calls even if they had been rejected.[20] In one extreme case even he thought that a boy was too mediocre to be accepted – but after multiple colleges had resisted a lobbying attempt by the family, eventually a place was found for him at Christ Church.[21]

Before hearing the result Rae wrote that 'If this boy gets into Oxford or Cambridge, it will be a triumph for the network.' And so it was. But it was a particular triumph because it was becoming so rare. The University was abolishing 'closed' scholarships and exhibitions, which were only available to candidates from a particular school; but in many cases their nature had already been changed so that, rather than guaranteeing places, they were supposed to be on an academic level with open scholarships (and in practice they were often used to 'trump' other colleges, in other words to persuade a strong applicant given a place without a scholarship at one college to choose instead another college offering a closed scholarship). Nonetheless, it was certainly felt that these awards did not have the same prestige – the most ambitious candidates tend to have tried to get open scholarships instead – and they were removed in 1985. St John's had defended their existence in the 1970s, but it seems that it had mainly used them for trumping: students 'not among the masterminds of the western world' seem to have stopped

---

19 Trevor-Roper (23 Mar. 1960) in Trevor-Roper (2006) pp. 303–4.
20 Rae (2009) pp. 19, 42, 77, 158, 199.
21 Ibid. pp. 244–5, 248.

finding a home at St John's in the 1960s.²² And again it was not a relative disadvantage: by the late 1970s the average college offered a slightly higher number of closed scholarships relative to its size than St John's did.²³

As with the comparison to University College's building scheme, there were similarities between St John's and Hertford. Both had young Fellows who wanted to shake things up. Both made an effort to reach out to state schools in particular – although privately the Fellows of St John's felt the conferences they put on for teachers at comprehensive schools weren't very successful.²⁴ But in other ways they were very different. St John's kept an eye on the Tanner Scheme and its precursors but did not join them, although several other colleges did. (It was, however, one of just five colleges which voted against them being ended.)²⁵ Access did improve, as Figure 4.8 shows, but there is no reason to think it improved by more than was typical for an Oxford college over this period. More accessible admissions do not explain the College's relative improvement.

Another potential reason for improved exam results would be if poor performers were removed before they could sit their exams – a situation not unheard of in Oxford. Fortunately this does not appear to have been the case at St John's, at least in the 1980s. (We do not have a Disciplinary Committee file before that, but as the 1980s were the College's most successful years academically, it is likely that such attempts were equally uncommon in earlier years.) Academic matters were a minor part of College discipline, which was mainly about dealing with the

22 SJC ADM IV.A.1.f; ADM IV.A.3.b.
23 SJC ADM IV.A.3.b.
24 SJC ADM IV.A.1.e.
25 Goldman (2018) pp. 12–13, 15.

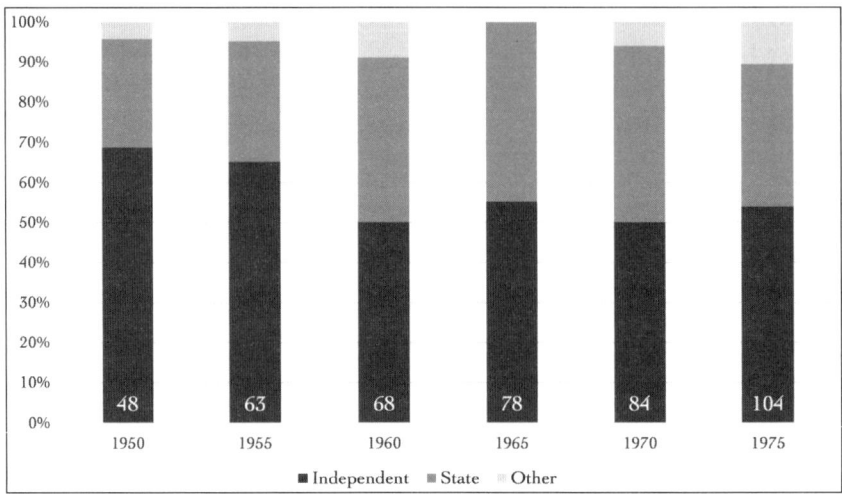

Figure 4.8: The Origin of Undergraduates Matriculating at St John's by School. Numbers at the base of the bars are the number of students matriculating that year.

aftermath of unruly undergraduate behaviour. (The most dramatic case was when a student at another college entered Front Quad wearing a beret and carrying a fake pistol. The porters, thinking it was a real gun, bravely rushed him and he was ejected from the College. The Disciplinary Committee noted that he was to be banned from re-entering St John's and that his confiscated beret was not to be returned, on the grounds that it was intimidating.)[26]

When there were genuine cases of academic problems, they seem to have been dealt with generously – although of course the archives give just one side of the story, and the file includes a letter from the JCR President who worried that the College had such a good reputation that tutors would expect too much

---

26 SJC ADM XXIII.B1.b.

of students: 'it would be extremely sad, not to say unjust, if an individual who contributes much to College, and who is clearly capable of a 3rd Class degree, should be sent down permanently because of unrealistic expectations'.[27] In fact from 1980 to 1991 just four students were permanently excluded: one had failed Prelims; two others had failed Prelims and another exam; and one had done very badly in an important area of the course. In another case there was pressure for a student to be sent down after very poor performance in Moderations and a Collection, but after protest he was allowed to stay and sit his Finals. An increase in ruthlessness on the part of the Fellows, therefore, can be ruled out.

From the University's perspective, the admission of women and the increase in accessibility for students without privileged backgrounds are the main stories in this period, and they were certainly the drivers of change. But St John's was not outstanding – either outstandingly good or outstandingly bad – in either case. As a result, these factors cannot explain why it began to outperform its collegiate peers.

Progression from the Mean

Is there a way to disentangle all these effects and quantify how important each one was? Honestly, probably not. Too many factors are important but have no good source of data: how do we measure the College's changing focus on admitting students based purely on ability, for example, without getting tangled up in students choosing to apply for other reasons? And do we have enough data points to reliably infer anything about the changes? Nonetheless, it is worth an attempt – if only to say that we know econometrics cannot provide us with the answers we want.

---

27 SJC ADM XXIII.B1.b.

Intellectual Capital

The strategy is to use the data we have (from 1955 to 1991) to estimate a model regressing undergraduate performance on data series related to the theories we have explored. Because the Norrington Table is just a ranking, it does not give the best insight into how the College's undergraduates were performing. A more useful measure is the underlying Norrington score; to account for the fluctuating difficulty of exams and grade inflation, the average Norrington score of the University in each year is subtracted from the College's Norrington score to produce an excess Norrington score. Since these scores are likely to be serially correlated, we find the difference between each year's performance and the previous year's performance and use these. The explanatory variables are real spending on tuition per undergraduate, access to accommodation throughout the degree, the admission of women, and the presence of President Southern. Spending is also likely to be serially correlated and so is also first differenced; the second and third explanatory series have more to do with admissions than exam performance and so have a three-year lag.[28]

The resulting regression has coefficients which make sense – the signs on tuition, accommodation and President Southern are all positive, while the sign on women is negative – but none are statistically significant, doubtless because we simply have too little data. One possibility is that we have a serious break point in our data series, perhaps reflecting the moment the College began to improve, but testing for this does not yield a significant

---

[28] Augmented Dickey-Fuller tests on the first differenced scores and spending series allow us to reject the hypothesis that either is non-stationary; both have p-values below 0.01.

result either.[29] A statistical analysis, therefore, is consistent with the rest of the evidence but not confirmatory.

Conclusion

So why did St John's go from being an academic basket case to one of Oxford's most successful colleges? The simplest explanation is that the Fellowship – or at least enough of it – was ready for change, which they showed by electing Richard Southern as President. Southern then went on to have a massive impact on the College, driving up standards through the force of his personality and judicious reforms. And it seems likely that this was the shock to the system the College needed: like others, once it had escaped a mediocre equilibrium its new status began to self-perpetuate (helped by a growing army of dedicated Tutorial Fellows).

But it is not quite that simple. First, Keith Thomas clearly played a crucial role in advocating for Southern to be elected. Perhaps he would have been chosen anyway, or perhaps someone else as good or better would have been selected. But it does not seem likely. Thomas's role, therefore, was potentially crucial. Second, it is not clear that Southern would have come had it not been for the College's wealth – as this allowed it to expand student numbers, provide full accommodation, and hire new Fellows. Southern wanted to improve education in Oxford, and that is much easier to do if you have the means.

Colleges can improve without buying their way to success: Hertford did; University did. But St John's probably wouldn't have. Unlike those other two colleges, there was no Tanner or

---

[29] The test used was a Chow test – full details of the tests undertaken and the regression results are available with the online data.

Albery in the centre driving change and pushing up standards. But there is no reason why there couldn't have been. Thomas seems to have attempted to rectify the problem by having the President play that role, and it worked very well: but would he have found sufficient support for that approach if the College hadn't had the money to buy all the things that smoothed its academic ascent? Probably he would not have. The path of least resistance was still to do what had always been done. It would not be fair to say that the College's finances *caused* it to become successful; but it is hard to believe that they were not a necessary ingredient.

5

ARRANGEMENTS AROUND THE FACT[1]

Could History Have Been Different?

They say (and I am glad they say)
It is so; and it may be so:
It may be just the other way,
I cannot tell. But this I know ...

Hilaire Belloc, *Dedicatory Ode*, 1910

Throughout this book, we have seen the rise, fall, and rise again of the St John's College endowment. We have traced how the College's academic fortunes rose, returning it to a status it had only enjoyed in the days of Laud. And I hope that you have emerged with a clear picture of these events, the structures which constrained and shaped them, and the data which allows us to reconstruct them.

In other words, I hope you have been deceived.

Nothing presented in this book so far is an accurate depiction of the data that underlies it. The accounts are a mess: with

---

[1] Taken from *Articulations for Keeping the Light In* edited by Rachel Long and Jacob Sam-La Rose, copyright © 2022. Reprinted by permission of Minying Huang (the author) and flipped eye publishing.

the exception of three years of limited data in 1872–4, probably hastily put together for commissioners enquiring about the College's financial state, we have nothing from 1868 until 1881. Nor is this merely a problem of the past: as I write these words it is an open question whether seventeen years of irreplaceable audits rest in a basement somewhere in North Oxford or spent their last moments on Earth going through a shredder.[2] In between, we have those documents that happened to survive – or were produced in the first place. Multiple 'accounts' are mentioned which show up once, or never, in the data. Valuations from the brokers and the auditors differ, even when based on the same methodology and purportedly taken on the same day.

What is true of the data is also true of its analysis. I think what I have written is accurate and as good an interpretation of the College's past as possible. But I may be wrong. There are documents in the archives – probably irrelevant, but I can't be sure of that – that I haven't had the time to see. There could be explanations I haven't thought of, or haven't given enough weight to.

'Counterfactual' reasoning has come in for a lot of criticism by historians, much of it along the following lines. The historian does not know what would have happened had things been different; their expertise is in assessing what *did* happen, and explaining that. They can assess the causes of things while recognising that events can be thrown off course by an 'accident': Cleopatra's nose, for example. But the purpose of history is to explain the rational, not the random. Counterfactuals are mere speculation and – as Richard Evans has argued – are suspicious

---

2 The audits – from 1986–2002 – ended up in the shredder. One of the Finance Office's stalwart staff seemed bemused at the idea that important financial information might be worth preserving.

Arrangements Around the Fact

as they are typically deployed by history's losers: 'most of the historians writing counterfactual history along these lines have been both politically and methodologically conservative ... rather than "what if," it's really little more than "if only."'[3]

There are two reasons to be sceptical of this rather conservative defence of historical methodology. The first is pleasingly abstract. How can we know that x caused z unless some change to x (and quite possibly y too – it can get complicated quickly) would have resulted in a change in z? Counterfactual scenarios can sharpen our thinking on this point. It is hard to imagine Europe not erupting into war early in the twentieth century, even had the not-so-fateful shot missed the Archduke: there were too many tensions and interlocking alliances for something like what did happen not to have ended up occurring. A story where these issues somehow resolved peacefully might seem like wishful thinking. And yet it is not so hard to imagine Madagascan schoolchildren taking notes as their teacher explains how the nuclear exchange that ended the Cold War and took out half the planet in the process was inevitable. There were too many tensions and interlocking alliances – not to mention previous near misses in tropical Cuban waters and cold Arctic skies – for something like what did happen not to have ended up occurring.[4] Suddenly we have a healthier scepticism as to whether the link between x and z is as solid as we thought.

There is also a more mundane reason to consider counterfactuals. We might be sure of the metaphysical link between x and z – but not be so sure whether it is relevant in this case. There is always more evidence to sift through, and it can always

---

3 Evans (2013) pp. 32, 62.
4 For a discussion of close calls in the Cuban Missile Crisis see Plokhy (2021) pp. 194, 203, 228, 259, 266–72, 285–6.

throw up new facts. I was confident that the plan to build an eighteen-storey tower block in North Oxford never came to fruition because it was opposed by the city council, as plans to deface historic skylines often are. But then I found a memo revealing the city council planning officer's support for the scheme, and this reminded me that the Engineering Department, which probably commits a greater crime against aesthetics than any tower block could hope to achieve, was built around the same time.[5] I still think that the tower block was always doomed, but I am less sure than I was: the powerful causal channel of 'the council will not allow architectural atrocities in a nice neighbourhood' has been weakened, even though it is no less valid in cases where the council *does* wish to intervene.

Our causal models are vulnerable to both these types of misspecification. One solution is a sensitivity analysis: an investigation to see how different the model's outcome looks when we feed in a range of different inputs. This is easy to do with a mathematical model – an economist can quickly run their model with different combinations of parameter values – but such models, let alone quantifiable parameters, are rarely applicable to history. Trying out different scenarios is more feasible and gives us a sense of how robust our explanations are to potential new evidence. Hopefully this will make us more confident; it will guard us against the kind of narrative overfitting that allows us to spin a satisfying story which can be blown over by a single stray fact.

All of this applies to the present book. So what counterfactuals do we need to think through?

---

5 SJC ADM II.C.2.

Arrangements Around the Fact

Just About Managing

The fateful decision to redevelop North Oxford, rather than divesting from it, left St John's exposed to the risk of leasehold enfranchisement. We have already seen that the political risk to the estate should have been obvious to the Fellows – but what if it was and they thought the redevelopment plans were so good that it made sense to roll the dice? There are two questions here: did running an estate in the way St John's did make sense; and how feasible were the specific plans it developed for Walton Manor?

There are two main reasons to own an estate, rather than an equivalent number of houses in different areas. One is that the costs of administering it may be lower: it's cheaper to have everything you're managing in one place where you can keep an eye on it. The second, discussed in Chapter 2, is the ability to internalise the externalities. For Walton Manor to have made sense as a redevelopment project, the benefit from internalised externalities would have had to be substantial.

Two other cases of estate management – almost polar opposites – provide a background against which to judge the College. The Howard de Walden Estate has owned Marylebone in London for centuries, operating with the standard London playbook: lease out buildings on long leases (many for 999 years); enforce covenants; collect the rewards. By the 1980s, however, Marylebone High Street – the centre of their property empire – was in poor shape. It was run down, unpopular, and failing to compete with nearby Oxford Street as a shopping experience. The estate's response was to redevelop it by buying up the leases they had granted and carefully selecting tenants to make it a destination: a variety of high-quality independent shops would offer customers a range of products they might not be able to find elsewhere, or could not find elsewhere in such pleasant surroundings. The plan was to create long-term value: when selecting anchor tenants they chose Waitrose over Tesco despite the latter offering 37.5 per cent more in rent because they thought it would offer a better experience for their customers and residents.[6]

Like the College's plans, the de Walden Estate's redevelopment scheme was almost knocked off course by local political factors – the council wanted to build social housing where they wanted the Waitrose to sit, among other issues. But the estate maintained a constant dialogue and got supportive councillors on side. And they were clear that although the council might offer 'co-operation and even some financial contributions', these would be limited and there would be other delays.[7]

Interestingly, the plans did not estimate the project's positive externalities, even though these provided much of the justification for completing it. Instead they simply noted that these were likely to be significant.[8] Little has changed: when I discussed how the Howard de Walden Estate and the Grosvenor Estate think about similar projects today, I was told that neither explicitly estimates the positive externalities which are likely to result, even though they are certainly taken into account.[9] This seems curious – development projects are unique and infrequent enough that it seems unlikely that even long experience will give an intuition of an ideal amount to spend, especially as there is a short-run cost and a long-run payoff. Furthermore, it seems like an area where economists could relatively easily

---

6 HdWE 7/3/10–11 (Aug. 1995).
7 Ibid. (Sept. 1993).
8 HdWE Andrew Ashenden File: Marylebone High Street: Regeneration (Box 256) Appendix 2 (1 Sept. 1995).
9 Private conversations.

and cheaply conduct an analysis. Nonetheless, this shows that it would be unreasonable to expect the Fellows of St John's to estimate positive externalities in this way, even though it is reasonable to think that they should have considered them.

In the end, the revitalisation of Marylebone High Street was a great success, increasing property values and allowing the area to bounce back much more quickly than it would have after the Great Recession. But going all-in on externalities was not the only way to make a success of an estate. Eton College, which owned Chalcots in North London, offers an alternative perspective. We have already seen how a mortgage had to be raised to compensate the Fellows for allowing the site to be leased for building houses, and their interest really does seem to have been limited to the financial benefits the land offered. The area became a byword for architectural blandness:

> complete anonymity ... for it can truthfully be said that not one solitary soul was ever really interested in what the physical, visible results would be. The Provost and Fellows may never even have seen the field they owned. They relied on the reports of their surveyor. The surveyor's sole interest was to lay out convenient roads, mark off building plots and take his fee.[10]

Investment in public goods seems to have been limited to the bare necessities, such as a church.

And yet Chalcots was 'an unusually successful suburb ... What generations of architects, surveyors, solicitors, and stewards strove vainly to achieve on the Bedford estate, Eton

---

10 Summerson (1963) p. 174.

College seems to have managed without really trying.'[11] F. M. L. Thompson argued that this was because it was in the right area: it was fated to succeed for topographical, rather than managerial, reasons.[12] There was little trouble in selling the houses and the estate even maintained its social character. Cannadine uses it as an example of his thesis in *Lords and Landlords*: the careful management activities he has patiently unearthed and lovingly laid out are almost irrelevant to the big economic questions; estates succeed or fail owing to 'the forces of the market, however much they might resemble 'putative planning authorities' in other respects.'[13] From this perspective, all the money St John's spent may as well have been poured down the drain.

What do these extremes show us? Neither is directly applicable to St John's: it did not have the capital available to the Howard de Walden Estate or the luxury of not caring what an estate on its doorstep looked like, as Eton did. But the fact that both were highly successful, while St John's was not, raises questions about whether its plans for redeveloping Walton Manor made any sense. Probably they did not. Insofar as North Oxford was a desirable destination, it probably would have been successful anyway without a lot of additional spending (as indeed it has ended up being, albeit partially thanks to the unforeseen growth of London). Unlike the Marylebone High Street project, St John's was not in constant contact with the council and seems to have assumed that it would fund measures such as road widening, which the council eventually made clear would not happen.[14] It was estimated that redevelopment would add

---

11 Olsen (1976) p. 247.
12 Thompson quoted in ibid. p. 248.
13 Cannadine (1980) p. 393.
14 SJC MUN V.C.67.2.

£31,000 per house in value (and maybe a bit more for nearby houses – but rent control would prevent them from benefiting from that). The cost was £94,000.[15] Certainly the sums could have been made to add up if the council had been generous, but this looks like wishful thinking from a plan which was never designed primarily as an investment.

Friends in High Places

In 1978, Trinity College, Cambridge faced the 'quasi-nationalisation' of Felixstowe Dock. Trinity did not own the dock, but it owned the land it was built on, and it was worried that the government buying it would result in the introduction of a 'restrictive dock labour scheme', as in other government-controlled docks in Britain, which would ruin its economic future.[16] Stopping the sale, however, required an Act of Parliament; and although Trinity joined other parties in giving evidence against the Bill at the committee stage, they were rebuffed. But Trinity would not take no for an answer, and responded by writing to every single Conservative and Liberal peer in the House of Lords. The Bill was defeated two to one, and Trinity put on a feast to celebrate – as well it might, for the dock continued to flourish and the land grew in value.

It's reasonable to doubt whether lobbying would have achieved anything for St John's. If, as I have argued, leasehold enfranchisement was the culmination of eighty years of protest and ill-feeling, why would we expect St John's to be able to resist that tide – especially when other colleges were not able to? There are a couple of caveats to this perspective, however. First, other

---

15 SJC MUN V.C.67.2.
16 This history is taken from Neild (2008) pp. 126–8.

lobbyists did manage to get changes to the Bill, albeit changes which the Cabinet was already sympathetic to. The changes St John's wanted would have been harder to achieve, but it seems unlikely that the optimal amount to have spent on lobbying was nothing. A suitably pathetic letter would have cost little to write. Second, St John's was not a natural target for the Bill. The focus was really on Wales, and unlike Western Ground Rents in Cardiff, St John's was not a faceless investment company. This would have meant relatively little if there was not some convenient way to separate St John's from the other estates. But such a route existed: the Bill could have excluded universities. Indeed Labour MP Evan Luard was so worried about this possibility that he called for the language in the Bill to be made more clear, so that St John's would *not* be able to claim that it was using the land for development.[17] It seems that backbenchers were worried that the government might give ground in the face of a determined lobbying effort.

They were right to be. While St John's did not engage in any lobbying, other groups did. Two Cambridge colleges – Trinity and St John's – sent a very detailed submission, noting both how the Act would hurt the University's ability to expand in Cambridge and how many aspects of it could lead to absurd consequences, such as a commercial building with a small flat being enfranchised at a knock-down price by the tenant.[18] The bursars later met with the Minister to press their case in person. They seem to have been unsuccessful – a Cabinet paper notes that investment property held by Oxbridge colleges would not be excluded from the Bill – but it is possible that the government

---

17 *Hansard.* HC Deb. Vol. 742 Col. 1375 (7 Mar. 1967).
18 SJC EST I.M.Main 318: North Oxford Estate: Leasehold Enfranchisement 1965–7 (5 June 1967).

held firm against attempts to raise the valuation limit in Oxford and Cambridge as a result.[19]

The restrained and technical lobbying by the Cambridge colleges was just one possible strategy. The Church Commissioners took advantage of the fact that the Prime Minister was himself, *ex officio*, a Church Commissioner, and so Lord Silsoe, another Church Commissioner, wrote to him – presumably with the intention of putting him in a difficult position.[20] This was as nothing, however, compared to the Grosvenor Estate's approach. Upon hearing that the limit on which houses would fall under the Bill had been scrapped, they wrote to Housing Minister Fred Willey to protest. There was no exploitation of tenants on their estate, they argued, but rather the opposite: 'there exist [in Pimlico] a substantial number of short-term tenancies, for the most part at uneconomic rates, and here again in Chester there are families who for generations have lived under the protection of the Grosvenor "umbrella". A forced sale … would be … nothing short of disastrous to the tenants concerned.' And the threatened damage was not limited to tenants. The letter went on to note that the estate was cross-subsidised, and losing the houses would mean that charitable work in the Highlands would have to come to an end: 'immediate dismissal of staff in Sutherlandshire employed in forestry, the bus services and road haulage'. Nor was there any beating about the bush: the workers had already been told 'that their continued employment depends upon the effect on the Estate of leasehold enfranchisement'.[21]

It is unclear how much of a role this threat played with the

---

19 NA HLG 29/723.
20 NA HLG 29/731 p. 197.
21 Ibid. pp. 191–3.

government – there was already pressure in the Cabinet to keep the limit – but it may have helped soften Willey's resistance to reinstating it. Certainly it made a splash in the Scottish press (for which the Grosvenors, rather unconvincingly, denied responsibility).[22] In any case Willey was sent a fawning letter after the limits were reinstated in the text of the Bill:

> I would like to express on behalf of the trustees of the Grosvenor Estate our appreciation of your reinstatement of the clause ... I am now able to reassure our employees in North-West Sutherland of the Grosvenor Estate's ability to continue to subsidise their employment, which I know will bring as great a sense of relief to them as it does to us.[23]

St John's was not in a position to publicly threaten that it would fire salt-of-the-earth labourers if it didn't get its way. Hopefully it would not have wanted to engage in strong-arming the government through such extraordinary means. And perhaps it thought that its scheme to evade the law by setting up a housing association would work better the less people knew about it – although this seems politically naïve. Certainly Garrard expressed surprise when the loophole was pre-emptively fixed – 'Who, indeed, would have imagined that Housing Associations would be popped back at the eleventh hour?' But he should not have been. The government was already aware of what St John's was trying to do and acting to stop it.[24] Even if they had not noticed, it seems unlikely that it would have done anything but bought a little time: Eton chose to avoid taking

---

22 NA HLG 29/731 p. 210.
23 Ibid. p. 212.
24 NA HLG 29/734.

advantage of a different loophole because, while it felt it was legally valid, 'it would probably lead to a great deal of adverse publicity and perhaps to political attack. In the second place, it would be almost certain to result in a change in the Law.'[25]

The possibility of successful lobbying – if only St John's had tried it – is tantalising. But the College's failure to lobby perhaps says more about its lack of sophistication in protecting its investments than it does about a possible future where its assets were protected through conversations behind closed doors. If Trinity and St John's in Cambridge could not persuade the government to establish a loophole for universities, it seems unlikely that St John's could have done much more.

Take the Money and Run

In Chapter 3, we established that the College could have foreseen leasehold enfranchisement – at least to the extent that it should have recognised it was a risk and taken action to protect itself. But how easy would it have been to withdraw capital from the estate? The obvious solution – forming a company and selling shares in it – had been vetoed by the Ministry of Agriculture. Selling the entire estate was not feasible: staff and Fellows lived on it; and a sophisticated buyer would have been even more aware of the risk from leasehold enfranchisement than was the College. Developers had already decided that the estate was not ready to be redeveloped. Thus the only option would have been relatively small-scale sales, perhaps to occupants who weren't gambling on leasehold enfranchisement occurring.

Eton was also considering redeveloping its Chalcots Estate in the early 1960s, and was also warned about the risk of leasehold

---

25 EC COLL/CHAL/1/1/10/2 (6 Mar. 1971) p. 2.

enfranchisement. Eton, however, took it much more seriously than St John's. There was a policy in place of selling houses to 'take capital out of the Estate' as early as 1957, and the school tentatively planned to extract £250,000 over five years (with the estate being valued at £2.5–3m).[26] In fact almost twice as much as that was realised in sales by 1961, and they kept going, as well as re-leasing houses which had fallen in on 21-year leases rather than new 99-year leases.[27] As late as 1963 they were still weighing the possibility of redevelopment but were clear that they would have to move quickly because 'If there is a change of Government in 1964 the College would probably be better placed to meet any changes in the law if the new rents were also ready being received.'[28]

Sidney Sussex College, Cambridge also had an estate. Rather like St John's, they had happened to own land – in its case in Cleethorpes – since 1616, which in the nineteenth century became ideal for building a seaside town.[29] The college had also used 99-year leases to develop the town and were vulnerable to leasehold enfranchisement. Unlike Eton they were deeply involved in the process, with Fellows visiting each year to see the situation on the ground and noting specific restrictions on permitted residents: 'the keeping of "hogs, boars, sows, pigs or other offensive beast" was forbidden'.[30] But when the investment no longer made sense, they were quick to act.

Unlike Eton, Sidney Sussex seem to have decided to get out of Cleethorpes because of the sort of arguments Richardson advanced: long leases weren't a sensible investment option for a

---

26 EC COLL/CHAL/1/1/6 (19 May 1958) pp. 1, 5; (14 May 1959) p. 2.
27 EC COLL/CHAL/1/1/9 (9 Dec. 1961).
28 EC COLL/CHAL/1/1/10/2 (13 July 1963) p. 2.
29 Ambler and Dowling (1996) p. 177.
30 Dowling (1997) p. 219; Ambler and Dowling (1996) p. 189.

college. The college's estates bursar presented a note to the Fellowship on the harm inflation did to ground rents in 1959, and by 1963 they were selling freeholds to householders. They had disposed of almost 30 per cent of them by 1968, at which point the rest were sold 'en bloc': presumably to some external buyer who must have paid a price reflecting the fact that leasehold enfranchisement had now been enacted.[31] The proceeds were invested in equities.

These examples – one in London, one in the north – reveal that there were ways to extract substantial amounts of capital from urban estates if it was a priority. One might imagine that the possibility of leasehold enfranchisement would cause markets to freeze up, but it seems that this was not the case until the White Paper was actually published. What is more, St John's *had* decided to sell large parts of North Oxford in 1960 – presumably Garrard would have explained to the Fellows that this was not practically possible if there had been no demand. It seems that much of the harm from leasehold enfranchisement could probably have been avoided: unless we were to find some reason why it was especially hard to dispose of property in North Oxford, there is every reason to think that, had the Fellowship acted when it was first warned in 1959, it could have protected the endowment from the disaster which struck it.

Foresight is 20/20

If it is true that leasehold reform was inevitable because long leaseholds made so little economic sense as contracts, this would surely apply to all leaseholds – not just those covered by the Leasehold Reform Act 1967. And this is what did in fact happen for houses: successive legislation weakened the restrictions in

---

[31] Ambler and Dowling (1996) pp. 192–3.

the 1967 Act until almost everyone had the right to enfranchise. Leasehold flats, on the other hand, did not see equivalent enfranchisement. Does this suggest that reform wasn't so inevitable after all? Alternatively, does it imply that leasehold flats will be enfranchised in the relatively near future?

In fact there was an attempt to do so. The Landlord and Tenant Act 1987 allowed leaseholders of flats to enfranchise, but it was so badly drafted that it was almost impossible for them to do so. The Leasehold Reform, Housing and Urban Development Act 1993 (which removed almost all limits on the enfranchisement of leasehold houses) created the right for flat owners to 'collectively enfranchise': if enough leaseholders in a building got together they could buy the freehold from the freeholder and then manage it themselves. But this was often difficult to arrange.

Efforts were also made to create an alternative form of tenure for flats. England was relatively unique internationally in having no legal mechanism for selling a freehold flat: for example the United States has the condominium and Australia has strata title. The problem is that living in a flat means that you inevitably have obligations to other members of the building, but such 'positive obligations' cannot survive the sale of property, so over time buildings with freehold flats would end up filled with flat owners who could not be made to contribute to repairs.[32] (The reason covenants could be enforced in North Oxford is because they were exclusively negative: 'don't harbour pigeons', etc.) A fundamentally new form of legal tenure was needed to get around this issue.

Commonhold was the Blair government's answer to this issue. The idea was that in a commonhold building each flat owner would own the freehold of their flat and have a defined

---

32 Clarke (1995) p. 487.

share of the ownership of the rest of the building, which would come with obligations. This would prevent the situation where some flat leaseholders would enfranchise and then take shares in the building, while other leaseholders did not join in. It all seems very sensible, which leaves the question of why it has not become popular.

Ten years after commonhold was introduced in 2002, Lu Xu investigated what impact the new form of tenure had had. His findings were disappointing. 'Fewer than 20 developments have been registered as commonhold in the 10 years since its commencement ... [there are] 16 commonhold developments in practice. There is hardly any word to describe the insignificance of such a number amongst thousands of new leasehold schemes being created every year.'[33] Hardly any solicitors were aware of how to set up a commonhold property, which made it less likely that any would be created in the future. This was all the more frustrating, Xu argued, because commonhold tended to work well – although since there have been so few, and the ombudsman who was supposed to police disputes does not exist, we probably cannot really say how robust commonhold is when dealing with disputes among residents. Ultimately he lays the blame for commonhold's failure with the rollout: it was badly marketed; potential buyers were worried that they might struggle to get mortgages or that, as directors of the commonhold associations, they might mess up the accounting; and there was no government support such as the creation of new commonhold buildings.

Today leasehold flats remain a problem, and for much the same reason that leasehold houses did. Just like the use by colleges of long leaseholds to build estates because they could not sell the land, the main reason that leasehold tenure is used are

---

33 Xu (2015) pp. 332, 335.

legal constraints, rather than because it makes economic sense. While ground rents can be a reasonable payment for the use of capital, and management companies can provide a good service for residents, both create opportunities for abuse enabled by the difficulty of residents getting together to resist unfair extractions. This is bad enough for existing buildings; it seems even more ridiculous to saddle new tower blocks with an antiquated form of tenure.

What does this mean for the future of leasehold reform? Trying to predict the future is always dangerous, because change rarely happens for a single reason: in a case such as leasehold flat reform, different parties have different things to gain and reasons to frustrate the process. If the issue isn't highly salient – and it is not – then it might be some time before the political situation is close enough to balance that it could make a difference (as it did when Labour held a four-seat majority in 1964). And the failure of commonhold shows that reform is not easy. But with these caveats in mind, we should expect reform to come to leasehold flats, and for the same reason that it came to leasehold houses: the legal structure is badly designed, creates opportunities for abuse, and predictably leads to frustration and regret. If it doesn't, then the force of the argument in Chapter 3 should be discounted accordingly.

Conclusion

Did the College's plans to redevelop Walton Manor make sense? Could lobbying have saved its investment in 1967? What about an attempt to sell? What does the future of leasehold reveal about the predictability of the risks St John's faced? And how do all these uncertainties alter the force of the arguments throughout this book?

Arrangements Around the Fact

This page intentionally left blank

EPILOGUE

The first chapter of this book could almost double as a history of drunkenness at St John's. Unfortunately financial history is not so amusing – although it is hopefully more interesting. Much of the College's financial history has been a history of avoidance: Fellows have just found it easier to concentrate on their own interests and let someone else get on with the job. We have seen the damage this can do, but there are other costs as well.

Chapter 4 investigated the extent to which wealth transformed the College's academic position. What is unarguable is the extent to which the endowment helps it today. Fellows and staff have better conditions and fewer worries. Students can get a richer education by travelling and presenting at conferences. Beautiful buildings can be preserved, restored, and augmented. What makes a college is the people, not the money – but there is a real sense in which the money brought the people together, and made their lives easier, happier, and more productive than they would otherwise have been. It is fashionable to disparage the richest American private universities as 'hedge funds with small schools attached'.[1] But much of that wealth is pumped back into research, and their international success shows the effect of this. Who wouldn't want to have a massively profitable hedge fund attached to their university? A cost of ignoring the role of finance, and those who work to

---

1 Hogan (5 Aug. 2022).

ensure it is deployed successfully, is that we underplay their contribution.

The second cost is that complacency can lead to disaster. St John's – like educational institutions as a whole – is far from unique in this respect, but a few examples show the damage that can be done. King's College, Cambridge grew rich from Keynes's judicious management of its already impressive endowment, ending up as rich as Trinity College.[2] After Keynes, King's returned to investing in real estate and then put the proceeds of a development project into the American stock market, only to experience Black Monday shortly afterwards.[3] Having bought at the top, they proceeded to sell at the bottom: there was no commitment to the long-term strategy of seeking exposure to American equities (in contrast to Keynes's own approach to US investment – he held firm when the market dropped in the late 1930s). Today King's has an endowment of £108m, lagging far behind not only its erstwhile Cantabrigian peers Trinity (£1,586m) and St John's (£695m), but also many other colleges.[4]

In Oxford, Magdalen College experienced mismanagement in a different sense. Decades of wealth meant that oversight of the domestic finances, and the state of the endowment, were limited. When Bill Johnson, a politics don, was elected senior bursar in 1980 he slowly realised the scale of the problem and began to clean out what turned out to be Augean stables of corruption. Magdalen was overspending on repairs (the same firm had been working for them for years with no competition, and workers were 'sick' half the time, working for other clients),

---

[2] Chambers, Dimson, and Foo (2015a) p. 128.
[3] Ibid. p. 146.
[4] King's College, Cambridge (2021) p. 53; Trinity College, Cambridge (2021) p. 12; St John's College, Cambridge (2021) p. 12.

Epilogue

staff (who drove expensive cars the college didn't even realise it technically owned and whose salaries were so generous that they refused to disclose them to the bursar), and had even lost control of its own car park: more than three-quarters of the spaces had been distributed to local businessmen as favours (and possibly in return for kickbacks).[5] After what Johnson describes as a Herculean effort by him and a group of Fellow workers, the situation stabilised – but Magdalen was in much worse shape than it needed to have been, and a lot of wealth had been squandered.

In all three cases – St John's; King's; Magdalen – a lack of scrutiny, enabled by a false sense of security, led to a significantly worse financial outcome than need have been the case. The presence of dedicated staff did not prevent that outcome (although it would have helped in Magdalen's case). Nor was it due to a failure to appoint a financial wizard who could make incredible bets and win vast sums for the college. Instead, relatively simple principles and aspects of good practice were ignored. It is surprisingly easy for things to go wrong even at a rich college. The stewardship and trusteeship which the Fellows on Governing Body exercise is an important duty that cannot be fully delegated. Nor, ultimately, do College officers benefit from avoiding scrutiny.

Fortunately things did turn around, managerially as well as academically. Indeed, since President Southern the College has gone from strength to strength. John Kendrew was followed as President by William Hayes, who as bursar had played a key role in improving the College's finances. The College grew as even more building took place and more Fellows, especially junior ones, were hired. Others went on to great things: having engineered a historian into the Presidency of St John's, Keith Thomas

---

5 Johnson (2015) pp. 196–200.

repeated the trick by becoming President of Corpus Christi College; and George Richardson, doubtless having resolved not to be a Cassandra again after the leasehold enfranchisement debacle, embarked on a successful career at the University Press and then as Warden of Keble.

The finances have also prospered. In 1980 John Kay, the College's Economics Fellow, became Investment Officer, supported by the investment sub-committee. The early results were solid if not spectacular: compared to a conventional portfolio invested 60 per cent in equities and 40 per cent in bonds, the College achieved a slightly lower real return. Then from 1985 to 2002 we are in the dark, as all the records have been destroyed (although we do know that the College came through the New Economy bubble relatively unscathed, having been sceptical of many of the claims made about the new companies being floated).

From 2003 onwards, however, we see serious outperformance, as Figure 6.1 shows. It is always difficult to establish counterfactuals in investing – who knows how the College would have done if other people had been running its money? The 60/40 portfolio is a relatively conventional choice, and from 2002 to 2021 it returned a fairly healthy 6.3 per cent per annum on average. The College's portfolio, on the other hand, returned an average of 11.9 per cent – and it had a better Sharpe ratio (1.47 vs. 0.52), suggesting that this was not just because it made a series of risky bets which happened to pay off.[6] The difference between the two portfolios is almost exactly £1bn. This is a theoretical total – St John's does not have that much money – as it includes income from the endowment which was spent,

---

6 The Sharpe ratio is a way of adjusting excess returns for risk, which is measured by volatility.

Epilogue

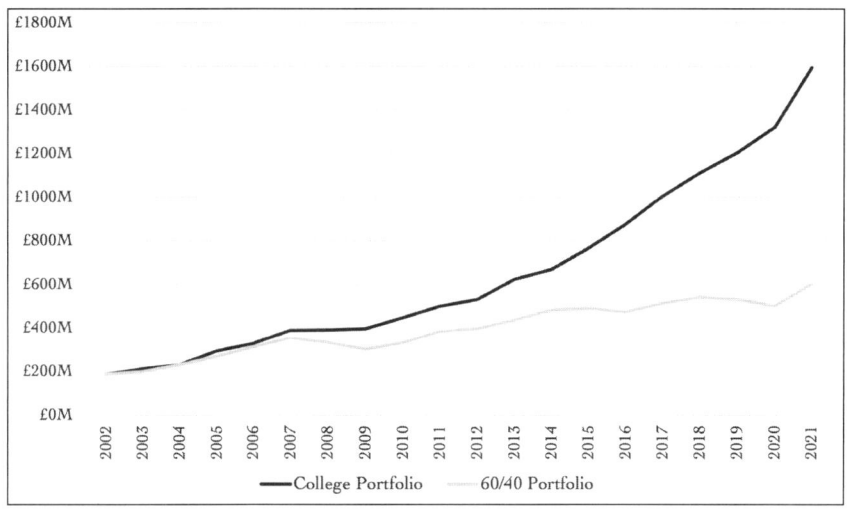

Figure 6.1: Investment Returns Assuming Reinvestment of All Profits

year by year, but which *could* have been saved and reinvested at the same rate of return.

By any measure, St John's has done very well. It is unlikely to do that well again. Fortunately it does not need to: it simply needs trustees who will act to preserve what they have been given – financially, academically, socially – and pass it on to those who follow them.

Appendix

HISTORY FROM BELOW

Following Laud's Tortoise Through the Archives

'At last we've got to the end of this ideal race-course! Now that you accept *A* and *B* and *C* and *D*, of course you accept *Z*.'
'Do I?' said the Tortoise innocently.
Lewis Carroll, 'What the Tortoise Said to Achilles', 1895

One important question – the most important question, really – is thus far unanswered. Did Front Quad once echo to the shuffling footsteps of Archbishop Laud's tortoise?

A surprising amount has been written about Laud's tortoise, and much of it is murky and contradictory. But we can be confident about a few things. First, we know that Laud joined St John's in 1589, where he was a scholar and then a Fellow. In 1611 he became President of St John's. He was then Bishop of St David's 1621–6, Bishop of Wells 1626–8, Bishop of London 1628–33, and finally Archbishop of Canterbury until his death. Second, there is in Lambeth Palace the shell of a tortoise which everyone agrees belonged to Archbishop Laud.

What kind of an animal was it? As its shell survives we can also be confident about this: it was a *Testudo graeca*, or spur-thighed tortoise. Despite the name this animal is found throughout North Africa and the Levant as well as Greece. Laud had acquired books and instruments from the Arab world, so it is possible he could have acquired a tortoise from there as well – but equally it could have had a different origin. It was certainly well studied, being the partial subject of two different scientific investigations.[1] But one of these, by Murray, was published in 1826, and he claims that Laud's tortoise died a natural death in 1753.[2] His research focuses on another episcopal tortoise: from it we learn that such creatures enjoyed a diet of seasonal fruits and berries and had fixed preferences: it relished an orange and 'positively rejected asparagus'.[3]

So how do we know anything about the tortoise? Its shell had three labels attached (now removed and in the Lambeth Palace archives).[4] These contradict each other. The first claims the tortoise was put into the garden at Lambeth by Laud in 1633 and died in 1753 'when it was unfortunately killed by the negligence of the gardener'. The second asserts that the tortoise made its debut in the garden in 1623 and remained there until 1730, when the gardener killed it. The third concurs with the second on the dates and adds that *another* tortoise was placed in the episcopal garden at Fulham by Laud in 1625 and died in 1723. It gives Murray as its source – which is curious, since Murray does mention the two tortoises but says that Laud's tortoise was placed in the garden at Fulham in 1628.[5] He asserts that the shell held at Lambeth was that of the other tortoise.

These dual tortoises and their duelling dates have caused

---

1 Murray (1826); Flower (1936).
2 Murray (1826) p. 169.
3 Ibid. p. 170.
4 LP MS 3407 (ff. 27–36).
5 Murray (1826) p. 168.

significant confusion for subsequent historians. It is all the more complicated because no one seems to have been writing remotely close to the time the tortoise was actually alive, let alone when Laud was. Flower, however, notes a report from 1779 asserting that there were two tortoises which both died in 1753 – plausibly the (anonymous) author knew the tortoises, or was drawing on an earlier source.[6]

We have one final clue, and it comes from the man who (re)discovered the tortoise. In his biography of Archbishop Laud, A. C. Benson writes of a record in Laud's diary that

> at the first touch of spring, his tortoise, then some sixty years old, that had been given him when at Oxford, used to issue from some secret crack and crawl painfully about. And, curiously enough, when the other day I was turning over some dusty relics–old parchment-deeds, faded stiff church-vestments, seals and crosses, that repose in an oak press in the Muniment-room,–there I came upon a tortoise-shell at the back of the shelf, on which was pasted a strip of paper, inscribed in antique brown characters, 'The Shell of a Tortoise, which was put into the Garden at Lambeth in the year 1633, where it remained till the year 1753, when it was unfortunately (or mortally) killed by the overflowing of the river.'[7]

Why is this merely a clue and not decisive evidence that the tortoise roamed St John's? Because Laud does *not* record such a thing in his diary. Not in his original diary, which now resides in the St John's library. Not in the published version of that diary.

---

6 Flower (1936) p. 6.
7 Benson (1887) p. 11.

And not even in the edited version put about by his enemies. Nor does Laud mention a tortoise in any of his other published writings (although in a letter he does thank a friend for her gift of a cat). But it does not follow that Benson was lying. He mentions the tortoise once, early in the biography, to set the scene: no part of his argument relies on it. It seems a strange thing to invent, especially as it is so easy to show that his citation is incorrect. Could he be misremembering where he read something that has not come down to historians today? It seems possible: in his preface he writes that

> it is the privilege of the biographer, who works on a more microscopic scale, to emphasize and drag to light all kinds of tiny relics, little papers annotated by friendly hands, flotsam and jetsam of the ages that accumulated fortuitously in muniment cupboards and archive chambers. Whether or not such search and such treasure-trove can give satisfaction to others remains to be seen. I can genuinely say that to me it has been a labour of love.[8]

We will probably never be certain whether Laud had his tortoise while he was at St John's: as with so many things, based on what we know it would not be surprising if he did and it would not be surprising if he did not. But we can say that it is plausible. St John's has been a home to many animals over the years: cats and dogs; foxes and badgers; peacocks and hedgehogs; harriers and pigeons. They enliven the gardens and delight the students, staff, and Fellows. But probably none has brought as much comfort to their human guardians as his tortoise did to Laud.

---

8 Benson (1887) p. xiii.

BIBLIOGRAPHY

1. This is the Record of John

Amhurst, N. *Strephon's Revenge: A Satire on the Oxford Toasts* (London: R. Francklin, 1724)

Amhurst, N. *Terræ-Filius; Or, the Secret History of the University of Oxford*, Vol. I (London: R. Francklin, 1726a)

Amhurst, N. *Terræ-Filius; Or, the Secret History of the University of Oxford*, Vol. II (London: R. Francklin, 1726b)

Anderson, J. 'The Operation of the Early Nineteenth-Century Property Market', *Construction History* Vol. 24 (2009) 63–81

Associated Press. 'Ghostly Doings at Magdalen College Since Excavation', *Associated Press* (17 Feb. 1987) <https://apnews.com/article/2a0f78c0c4b4a8d8acfe88ec2b7e5a30> (accessed 27 July 2022)

Ball, O. H. (ed.) *Sidney Ball: Memories and Impressions of 'An Ideal Don'* (Oxford: Basil Blackwell, 1923)

Bellingham, L. *Oxford: The Novel* (London: Nold Jonson Books, 1981)

Brockliss, L. W. B. (ed.) *Magdalen College Oxford: A History* (Oxford: Magdalen College, 2008)

Brockliss, L. W. B. *The University of Oxford: A History* (Oxford: OUP, 2016)

Carey, J. *The Unexpected Professor: An Oxford Life in Books* (London: Faber & Faber, 2015)

Chambers, D., Spaenjers, C. and Steiner, E. 'The Rate of Return on Real Estate: Long-Run Micro-Level Evidence', *Review of Financial Studies*, Vol. 34 (2021) 3572–607

Childs, J. 'The Restoration Army 1660–1702' in Chandler, D. G. and Beckett, I. (eds.) *The Oxford History of the British Army* (Oxford: Oxford University Press, 1996) 46–66

College Record (1913–1993)

Colvin, H. M. 'The Building of St Bernard's College', *Oxoniensa* Vol. 24 (1959) 37–48

Costin, W. C. *The History of St John's College, Oxford 1598–1860* (Oxford: Clarendon Press, 1958)

Coulson, C. 'Hierarchism in Conventual Crenellation: An Essay in the Sociology and Metaphysics of Medieval Fortification', *Medieval Archaeology* Vol. 26, No. 1 (1982) 69–100

Darwall-Smith, R. *A History of University College, Oxford* (Oxford: OUP, 2008)

Day, P. *On the Cucumber Tree* (Glasgow: The Grimsay Press, 2012)

Dibdin, T. F. *Reminiscences of a Literary Life* (London: John Major, 1836)

Dowling, A. 'The Corporate Landowner in Town Development, with Particular Reference to Grimsby and Cleethorpes c.1800–c.1900', Unpublished doctoral thesis (Hull: University of Hull, 1997)

Dunbabin, J. P. D. 'College Estates and Wealth 1660–1815' in Sutherland, L. S. and Mitchell, L. G. (eds.) *The History of the University of Oxford*, Vol. V (Oxford: Clarendon Press, 1986) 269–308

Dunbabin, J. P. D. 'Finance and Property' in Brock, M. G.

and Curthoys, M. C. (eds.) *The History of the University of Oxford, Part I*, Vol. VI (Oxford: Clarendon Press, 1997) 375–436

Faber, G. *Notes on the History of the All Souls Bursarships and the College Agency* (Plymouth: Latimer Trend & Co., 1950)

Faught, C. B. *The Oxford Movement: A Thematic History of the Tractarians and Their Times* (University Park, PA: Pennsylvania State University Press, 2004)

Fletcher, T. W. 'The Great Depression of English Agriculture 1873–1896', *Economic History Review* Vol. 13, No. 3 (1961) 417–32

Gibbon, E.; Morley, H. (ed.) *Memoirs of Edward Gibbon* (London: Routledge and Sons, 1891)

Gilbert, W. S. and Sullivan, A. *Patience, or, Bunthorne's Bride* (1881) <https://gsarchive.net/patience/patienclib.pdf> (accessed 23 Aug. 2022)

Graves, R. *Goodbye to All That* (London: Penguin, 1960)

Green, V. H. H. *Oxford Common Room: A Study of Lincoln College and Mark Pattison* (London: Edward Arnold Ltd, 1957)

Hansard. HC Deb. Vol. 784 Cols. 737–71 (22 May 1969)

Hardy, T. *Jude the Obscure* (London: Osgood, McIlvaine, & Co., 1895)

Harrison, B. (ed.) *The History of the University of Oxford: Volume VIII: The Twentieth Century* (Oxford: Clarendon Press, 1994)

Hearne, T.; Rannie, D. W. (ed.) *Remarks and Collections of Thomas Hearne*, Vol. V (Oxford: Clarendon Press, 1901)

Heygate, W. E. *Godfrey Davenant at College* (London: Joseph Masters, 1849)

High Court of Justice. *Probate: The Reverend James Bellamy* (21 Dec. 1909)

Hinchcliffe, T. *North Oxford* (London: Yale University Press, 1992)

Historical Manuscripts Commission. *Report on the Manuscripts of His Grace the Duke of Portland, Preserved at Welbeck Abbey*, Vol. VII (London: HMSO, 1901)

Hutton, W. H. *S. John Baptist College* (London: F. E. Robinson, 1898)

Jones, J. *Balliol College: A History* (Oxford: OUP, 2005)

Kidd, H. *The Trouble at L.S.E., 1966–1967* (London: OUP, 1969)

Knox, V. *Essays Moral and Literary*, Vol. I (New York: T. Allen, 1793)

Laud, W. *The Works of Archbishop Laud*, Vol. VII (Oxford: John Henry Parker, 1860)

Mabbott, J. D. *Oxford Memories* (Oxford: Thornton's, 1986)

Mallock, W. H. *The New Republic* (London: Chatto & Windus, 1906)

Naiman, E. 'Their Mutual Friend: On the Trail of the Woman Who Introduced Dickens to Dostoevsky', *Times Literary Supplement* (12 Apr. 2013) 16–21

Neild, R. *The Financial History of Cambridge University* (London: Thames River Press, 2012)

Nichols, B. *Patchwork* (New York: Henry Holt & Company, 1922)

Offer, A. *The First World War: An Agrarian Interpretation* (Oxford: Clarendon Press, 1991)

Oman, C. *Memories of Victorian Oxford* (London: Methuen & Co., 1941)

Pattison, M. *Memoirs* (London: Macmillan & Co., 1885)

Prideaux, H., Thompson, E. M. (ed.) *Letters of Humphrey Prideaux to John Ellis* (London: Nichols and Sons, 1875)

Purdue, A. W. 'An Oxford College, Two Parishes and a

Tithe-Farmer: The Modernisation of Tithe Collection', *Rural History* Vol. 8, No. 1 (1997) 1–19

Rae, J. *The Old Boys' Network: A Headmaster's Diaries, 1972–1988* (London: Short Books, 2009)

Reid, S. *All the King's Armies: A Military History of the English Civil War 1642–1651* (Staplehurst: Spellmount, 1998)

Shadwell, L. L. *Enactments in Parliament Specially Concerning the Universities of Oxford and Cambridge, the Colleges and Halls Therein, and the Colleges of Winchester, Eton & Westminster*, Vol. IV (Oxford: Clarendon Press, 1912)

Simpson, A. W. B. *Reflections on 'The Concept of Law'* (Oxford: OUP, 2021)

Skinner, S. A. 'Heygate, William Edward' *Oxford Dictionary of National Biography* (2004)

Smith, A. *An Enquiry into the Nature and Causes of the Wealth of Nations*, Vol. II (London: Strachan and Cadell, 1776)

Stevenson, W. H. and Salter, H. E. *The Early History of St John's College, Oxford* (Oxford: Clarendon Press, 1939)

Trevor-Roper, H. *Archbishop Laud 1573–1645* (London: MacMillan & Co., 1962)

Trevor-Roper, H.; Murray, J. (ed.) *The Letters of Mercurius* (London: William Clowes and Sons, 1970)

Tuckwell, W. *Pre-Tractarian Oxford: A Reminiscence of the Oriel 'Noetics'* (London: Smith, Elder, & Co., 1909)

Tuckwell, W. *Reminiscences of Oxford* (London: Smith, Elder & Co., 1907)

Turner, M. 'Corporate Strategy or Individual Priority? Land Management, Income and Tenure on Oxbridge Agricultural Land in the Mid-Nineteenth Century', *Business History* Vol. 42, No. 4 (2000) 1–26

Tyack, G. *Modern Architecture in an Oxford College: St John's College 1945–2005* (Oxford: OUP, 2005)

Universities Commission. *Report of the Commissioners Appointed to Inquire into the Property and Income of the Universities of Oxford and Cambridge, and of the Colleges and Halls Therein; Together with Returns and Appendix*, Vol. I (London: HMSO, 1874)
Waugh, E. *A Little Learning* (London: Penguin, 1983)
Waugh, E. *Brideshead Revisited* (London: Penguin, 2000)
Waugh, E. *Vile Bodies* (London: Chapman & Hall, 1930)
Wood, A. A.; Bliss, P. (ed.) *Athenae Oxonienses*, Vol. III (London: Baldwin, Craddock, and Joy, 1817)

2. Et in Arcadia Ego

Avrahampour, Y. '"Cult of Equity": Actuaries and the Transformation of Pension Fund Investing, 1948–1960', *Business History Review* Vol. 89, No. 2 (2015) 1–24
Butler, D. 'Reflections on British Elections and Their Study', *Annual Review of Political Science* Vol. 1 (1998) 451–64
Cannadine, D. *The Decline and Fall of the British Aristocracy* (London: Yale University Press, 1990)
Chambers, D., Dimson, E., and Foo, J. 'Keynes the Stock Market Investor: A Quantitative Analysis', *Journal of Financial and Quantitative Analysis* Vol. 50, No. 4 (2015b) 843–68
Chambers, D., Dimson, E., and Kaffe, C. 'Seventy-Five Years of Investing for Future Generations', *Financial Analysts Journal* Vol. 76, No. 4 (2020) 5–21
Chambers, D., Spaenjers, C. and Steiner, E. 'The Rate of Return on Real Estate: Long-Run Micro-Level Evidence', *Review of Financial Studies*, Vol. 34 (2021) 3572–607
Christensen, M. M. 'On the History of the Growth-Optimal Portfolio' in Györfi, L., Ottucsák, G., and Walk, H. (eds.)

Machine Learning for Financial Engineering (London: Imperial College Press, 2012) 1–79

Cornford, F. M. *Microcosmographica Academica: Being a Guide for the Young Academic Politician* (Cambridge: Bowes and Bowes, 1908)

Davies, A. *The City of London and Social Democracy: The Political Economy of Finance in Britain, 1959–1979* (Oxford: OUP, 2017)

Dimson, E. and Acharya, S. *Endowment Asset Management: Investment Strategies in Oxford and Cambridge* (Oxford: OUP, 2007)

Dunbabin, J. P. D. 'Finance Since 1914' in Harrison, B. (ed.) *The History of the University of Oxford: Volume VIII: The Twentieth Century* (Oxford: Clarendon Press, 1994) 639–82

Dunbabin, J. P. D. 'Oxford and Cambridge College Finances, 1871–1913', *Economic History Review* Vol. 28, No. 4 (1975) 631–47

Fisher, I. *The Theory of Interest* (New York: The Macmillan Company, 1930)

Ford, M. C. and Kay, J. A. 'Psychology is Fundamental: The Limitations of Growth-Optimal Approaches to Decision Making under Uncertainty' (17 Jan. 2023). Available at SSRN: <https://ssrn.com/abstract=4140625> (accessed 1 Feb. 2023)

Goetzmann, W. N., Griswold, J., and Tseng, Y.-F. (A.) 'Educational Endowments in Crisis', *Journal of Portfolio Management* Vol. 36, No. 4 (2010) 112–23

Heinemann, K. 'Investment, Speculation and Popular Stock Market Engagement in 20th-Century Britain', *Archiv für Sozialgeschichte* Vol. 56 (2016) 249–72

Hinchcliffe, T. *North Oxford* (London: Yale University Press, 1992)

Kay, J. A. and King, M. A. *Radical Uncertainty* (London: The Bridge Street Press, 2020)

Kemp, P. *Private Renting in Transition* (Plymouth: Chartered Institute of Housing, 2004)

Keynes, J. M.; Moggridge, D. (ed.) *The Collected Writings of John Maynard Keynes: Volume XII* (Cambridge: Cambridge University Press, 2013)

King's College, Cambridge. *Statutes 1926–27* (1927)

Mabbott, J. D. *Oxford Memories* (Oxford: Thornton's, 1986)

Maltby, J. et al. 'The Evidence for "Democratization" of Share Ownership in Great Britain in the Early Twentieth Century' in Green, D. R. (ed.) *Men, Women, and Money: Perspectives on Gender, Wealth, and Investment 1850–1930* (Oxford: OUP, 2011) 184–206

Markowitz, H. 'Portfolio Selection', *Journal of Finance* Vol. 7, No. 1 (1952) 77–91

Markowitz, H. 'The Early History of Portfolio Theory: 1600–1960', *Financial Analysts Journal* Vol. 55, No. 4 (1999) 5–16

McCallum, R. B. 'Oxford and the Financial Crisis', *Oxford Magazine* (15 Oct. 1931) 13–4

McCallum, R. B. *Public Opinion and the Last Peace* (London: OUP, 1944)

McCallum, R. B. and Readman, A. *The British General Election of 1945* (Oxford: OUP, 1947)

Moggridge, D. E. *Maynard Keynes: An Economist's Biography* (London: Routledge, 1992)

Neild, R. *Riches and Responsibility: The Financial History of Trinity College, Cambridge* (Cambridge: Granta Editions, 2008)

Neild, R. *The Financial History of Cambridge University* (London: Thames River Press, 2012)

Rogers, E. 'The Finances of St John's College During the Twentieth Century' in Linehan, P. (ed.). *St John's College, Cambridge: A History* (Woodbridge: The Boydell Press, 2011) 676–94

Rutterford, J., Green, D. R., Maltby, J. and Owens, A. 'Who Comprised the Nation of Shareholders? Gender and Investment in Great Britain, c. 1870–1935', *Economic History Review* Vol. 64, No. 1 (2011) 157–87

St John's College. *Statutes of St. John Baptist College* (Oxford: Clarendon Press, 1956)

3. The Avalanche

Berlin, I.; Hardy, H. and Holmes, J. (eds.) *Enlightening: Letters 1946–60* (London: Pimlico, 2011)

Cannadine, D. *Lords and Landlords: The Aristocracy and the Towns 1774–1967* (Leicester: Leicester University Press, 1980)

Chase, M. 'Chartism and the Land: "The Mighty People's Question"' in Cragoe, M. and Readman, P. (eds.) *The Land Question in Britain, 1750–1950* (Basingstoke and New York: Palgrave Macmillan, 2010) 57–73

Collier, P. *The Future of Capitalism: Facing the New Anxieties* (London: Penguin, 2018)

Country Life. 'Land Nationalisation Revived', *Country Life* Vol. 130, No. 3367 (14 Sept. 1961) 544

Crossman, R. *The Diaries of a Cabinet Minister: Volume One: Minister of Housing 1964–66* (London: Hamish Hamilton, 1975)

Crossman, R. *The Diaries of a Cabinet Minister: Volume Two:*

Lord President of the Council and Leader of the House of Commons, 1966–68 (London: Hamish Hamilton, 1976)

Dalyell, T. *Dick Crossman: A Portrait* (London: Weidenfeld & Nicolson, 1989)

Davenport, R. J. 'Urbanization and Mortality in Britain, c. 1800–50', *Economic History Review* Vol. 73, No. 2 (2020) 455–85

Davey, M. 'Long Residential Leases: Past and Present' in Bright, S. (ed.) *Landlord and Tenant Law: Past, Present and Future* (London: Bloomsbury, 2006) 147–69

Davey, M. 'The Onward March of Leasehold Enfranchisement', *Modern Law Review* Vol. 57, No. 5 (1994) 773–87

Davies, J. *Cardiff and the Marquesses of Bute* (Cardiff: University of Wales Press, 1981)

Englander, D. *Landlord and Tenant in Urban Britain 1838–1918* (Oxford: Clarendon Press, 1983)

Haley, M. 'Compensation for Tenants' Improvements: A Valediction?', *Legal Studies* Vol. 11, No. 2 (1991) 119–30

Hansard. HC Deb. Vol. 644 Cols. 401–69 (12 July 1961)

Hansard. HC Deb. Vol. 668 Cols. 1621–1721 (7 Dec. 1962)

Hansard. HC Deb. Vol. 748 Cols. 1470–1539 (20 June 1967)

Hansard. HC Deb. Vol. 784 Cols. 737–71 (22 May 1969)

Hansard. HL Deb. Vol. 180 Cols. 512–59 (18 Feb. 1953)

Hinchcliffe, T. 'Gentrification: The Case of Canonbury, 1850 to 1975' in Guillery, P. and Kroll, D. (eds.) *Mobilising Housing Histories: Learning From London's Past for a Sustainable Future* (London: RIBA Publishing, 2017) 107–21

Hinchcliffe, T. *North Oxford* (London: Yale University Press, 1992)

Bibliography

Honeyman, V. *Richard Crossman: A Reforming Radical of the Labour Party* (London: I. B. Tauris & Co., 2007)

The Labour Party, *Signposts for the Sixties* (1963)

Liberal Land Committee. *Towns and the Land: Urban Report of the Liberal Land Committee, 1923–25* (London: Hodder & Stoughton, 1925)

Marías, J.; Jull Costa, M. (trans.) *All Souls* (London: Harvill, 1992)

Offer, A. *Property and Politics 1860–1914: Landownership, Law, Ideology and Urban Development in England* (Cambridge: CUP, 1981)

Ortolano, G. 'Begrudging Neoliberalism: Housing and the Fate of the Property-Owning Social Democracy' in Davies, A., Jackson, B., and Sutcliffe-Braithwaite, F. (eds.) *The Neoliberal Age? Britain Since the 1970s* (London: UCL Press, 2021) 319–35

Places of Worship (Enfranchisement) Act (1920) c. 56

Quinault, R. 'London and the Land Question, c. 1880–1914' in Cragoe, M. and Readman, P. (eds.) *The Land Question in Britain, 1750–1950* (Basingstoke and New York: Palgrave Macmillan, 2010) 167–80

Thompson, F. M. L. 'Epilogue: The Strange Death of the English Land Question' in Cragoe, M. and Readman, P. (eds.) *The Land Question in Britain, 1750–1950* (Basingstoke and New York: Palgrave Macmillan, 2010) 257–70

Thompson, F. M. L. 'Land and Politics in England in the Nineteenth Century', *Transactions of the Royal Historical Society* Vol. 15 (1965) 23–44

4. A Little Learning

Carey, J. *The Unexpected Professor: An Oxford Life in Books* (London: Faber & Faber, 2015)

Goldman, L. *The 'Tanner Scheme' at Hertford College: Widening Access, Reforming Oxford, 1965–85* (2018) <https://www.hertford.ox.ac.uk/wp-content/uploads/2019/10/The-Tanner-Scheme-Research-Project-PDF.pdf> (accessed 22 Nov. 2022)

Grahame, K. *The Wind in the Willows* (London: Methuen, 1908)

Lowe, J. *The Warden: A Portrait of John Sparrow* (London: HarperCollins, 1998)

Polybius; Scott-Kilvert, I. (trans.), Walbank, F. W. (ed.) *The Rise of the Roman Empire* (Harmondsworth, Middlesex: Penguin, 1979)

Rae, J. *The Old Boys' Network: A Headmaster's Diaries, 1972–1988* (London: Short Books, 2009)

Trevor-Roper, H.; Davenport-Hines, R. (ed.) *Letters from Oxford* (London: Weidenfeld & Nicolson, 2006)

Trevor-Roper, H.; Davenport-Hines, R. and Sisman, A. (eds.) *One Hundred Letters from Hugh Trevor-Roper* (Oxford: OUP, 2014)

Tyack, G. *Modern Architecture in an Oxford College: St John's College 1945–2005* (Oxford: OUP, 2005)

Wassarman, P. M. *A Place in History: The Biography of John C. Kendrew* (Oxford: OUP, 2020)

5. Arrangements Around the Fact

Ambler, R. W. and Dowling, A. 'The Growth of Cleethorpes and the Prosperity of Sidney, 1616–1968' in Beales, D. E. D. and Nisbet, H. B. (eds.) *Sidney Sussex College Cambridge:*

Bibliography

Historical Essays in Commemoration of the Quatercentenary (Woodbridge: Boydell, 1996) 177–94

Belloc, H. 'Dedicatory Ode' in *Verses* (London: Duckworth & Co., 1910) 55–62

Cannadine, D. *Lords and Landlords: The Aristocracy and the Towns 1774–1967* (Leicester: Leicester University Press, 1980)

Clarke, D. N. 'Commonhold: A Prospect of Promise', *Modern Law Review* Vol. 58, No. 4 (1995) 486–504

Dowling, A. 'The Corporate Landowner in Town Development, with Particular Reference to Grimsby and Cleethorpes c.1800–c.1900' (1997) <https://ethos.bl.uk/OrderDetails.do?uin=uk.bl.ethos.265133> (accessed 30 Nov. 2022)

Evans, R. J. *Altered Pasts: Counterfactuals in History* (Waltham, MA: Brandeis University Press, 2013)

Hansard. HC Deb. Vol. 742 Cols. 1271–395 (7 Mar. 1967)

Huang, M. 'Arrangements Around the Fact' in Long, R. and Sam-La Rose, J. (eds.) *Articulations for Keeping the Light In* (London: flipped eye publishing, 2022)

Neild, R. *Riches and Responsibility: The Financial History of Trinity College, Cambridge* (Cambridge: Granta Editions, 2008)

Olsen, D. J. *The Growth of Victorian London* (London: B. T. Batsford, 1976)

Plokhy, S. *Nuclear Folly: A New History of the Cuban Missile Crisis* (London: Allen Lane, 2021)

Summerson, J. 'Urban Forms' in Handlin, O. and Burchard, J. (eds.) *The Historian and the City* (Boston, MA: The MIT Press and the Harvard University Press, 1963) 165–76

Xu, L. 'Commonhold Developments in Practice' in Barr, W.

(ed.) *Modern Studies in Property Law* (London: Hart Publishing, 2015) 331–50

Epilogue

Chambers, D., Dimson, E., and Foo, J. 'Keynes, King's, and Endowment Asset Management' in Brown, J. R. (ed.) *How the Financial Crisis and Great Recession Affected Higher Education* (Chicago, IL: University of Chicago Press, 2015a) 127–50

Hogan, D. M. 'Ruling Class in Session: On Charlie Eaton's "Bankers in the Ivory Tower"', *Los Angeles Review of Books* (5 Aug. 2022) <https://lareviewofbooks.org/article/ruling-class-in-session/> (accessed 20 Sept. 2022)

Johnson, R. W. *Look Back in Laughter: Oxford's Post-War Golden Age* (Newbury, Berkshire: Threshold Press, 2015)

King's College, Cambridge. *Annual Report and Accounts* (2021)

St John's College, Cambridge. *Annual Report and Financial Statements* (2021)

Trinity College, Cambridge. *Annual Report of the Trustees and Financial Statements for the Year Ended 30 June 2021* (2021)

Appendix: History from Below

Benson, A. C. *Archbishop Laud: A Life* (London: Kegan Paul, Trench & Co., 1887)

Carroll, L. 'What the Tortoise Said to Achilles', *Mind* Vol. 4, No. 14 (1895) 278–80

Flower, S. S. 'Further Notes on the Duration of Life in Animals. – III. Reptiles', *Proceedings of the Zoological Society of London* (1936) 1–39

Laud, W. St John's College Library. MS 317
Laud, W. *The Works of Archbishop Laud*, Vol. VII (Oxford: John Henry Parker, 1860)
Murray, J. *Experimental Researches on the Light and Luminous Matter of the Glow-worm, the Luminosity of the Sea, the Phenomena of the Chameleon, the Ascent of the Spider into the Atmosphere, and the Torpidity of the Tortoise, &c.* (Glasgow: W. R. McPhun, 1826)

Data and Archives

The data gathered during the project, including the data used for the figures, is available at https://doi.org/10.5281/zenodo.7535606

Additional Sources of Data

Dimson, E., Marsh, P., and Staunton, M. *Credit Suisse Global Investment Returns Yearbook 2020* (Zurich: Credit Suisse Research Institute, 2020)
Global Financial Data. 'GFD Indices United Kingdom USD Bond Return Index' (2022)
Global Financial Data. 'GFD Indices United Kingdom USD Stock Return Index' (2022)
Global Financial Data. 'United Kingdom 1-Year Government Note Yield' (2022)
University of Oxford. *Abstracts of the Accounts of the Curators of the University Chest and of University Institutions, Together with the Accounts of the ... Colleges* (Oxford: Clarendon Press, 1883–1980). (Note that footnotes assume the college referenced is St John's unless explicitly noted.)
Eton College Archive. Abbreviation EC

Howard de Walden Estate Archive. Abbreviation HdWE
Lambeth Palace Archive. Abbreviation LP
National Archives. Abbreviation NA
St John's College Archive. Abbreviation SJC

INDEX

A
Academic standards
  at Oxford 5, 11, 14–16,
    18–20, 23–4, 44, 96
  at St John's 6, 19, 25, 38–40,
    44–6, 48, 68, 139, 141–4,
    150, 165–6, 187
Act of Parliament
  Agriculture Act 1958
  Landlord and Tenant Act
    1927 119, 126
  Landlord and Tenant Act
    1954 126
  Landlord and Tenant Act
    1987 182
  Leasehold Property
    (Repairs) Act 1938 126
  Leasehold Property
    (Temporary Provisions)
    Act 1951 126
  Leasehold Reform Act
    1967 57–9, 89, 111–12, 114,
    130–2, 134, 151, 176–8, 182
  Leasehold Reform Bill 1962
    119
  Leasehold Reform,
    Housing and Urban
    Development Act 1993
    182
  Places of Worship
    (Enfranchisement) Act
    1920 125, 129
  Private Act (St John's) 1, 26,
    34
  Rent Act 1965 131
  Rents and Mortgage
    Interest Restriction Act
    1915 114
  University and Colleges
    Estates Act 1858 28, 32
Admissions 12–14, 46, 48,
  151–2, 154, 157–9, 163–4
  by school 157–9, 161
  not a function of
    academic ability 46–7,
    147, 157

Agricultural Depression 33–4, 41
Albury, John 147–8, 166
Alcohol 33, 61
  as bottled wealth 18, 44, 72, 82–3
  excessive consumption of 11–12, 16, 20, 38, 150, 187
All Souls College 31n92, 37, 47, 62–4, 75, 143–4, 154
Amhurst, Nicholas 13–16
Attlee family 128
Auditors 57

B
Bagley Wood 78
Ball, Sidney 39–41
Balliol College 3, 20, 23, 32, 48
  reject from 45, 158
  rejected by 63
Beehive 18, 46, 48, 62
Bellamy, James 40–1
Bequest, *see* Gifts
Berlin, Isaiah 127–8, 144
Bidder, Henry Jardine 33
Black Monday 188
Bloomsbury 117
Brasenose College 156n12
Brett, Lionel 50, 102n58, 104
British Academy 46, 141
Broadhurst, Henry 124
Brooks, Henry 132
Bruno, Giordano 5
Building leases, *see* 99-year leases
Bute family 117–18, 132

C
Callaghan, James 127, 129, 132
Campion, Edmund 5
Canterbury Quadrangle 6–7
Cardiff 117–18, 121, 127, 129–30, 132, 176
Carey, John 47, 68, 148, 150, 157
Carr, Ralph 29
Catholics 98
  persecution of 5, 38
Cats 196
Chalcots Estate 36–7, 173–4, 179–80
Charles I 7, 9
Christ Church 13, 49, 75, 156
  will take anyone sufficiently rich 159–60
Church Commissioners 106, 131, 177
Churchill, Randolph 124
Cistercians, *see* St Bernard's College
City council 54, 88, 100, 102, 105–6, 116, 170, 174
  town plan 48–50, 105

Index

Civil War 9
Clarke, Richard 38
Cleethorpes 180
Cluttons 53–4, 89, 109, 136
Commission
  into University of Oxford (1850) 24
  into University of Oxford (1872) 168
  on the Housing of the Working Classes, Royal 123–4
Commonhold 182–4
Computus Annus 26–7
Conservative Party 95, 115, 124, 127, 132, 134
Copleston, Edward 31n92, 32
Corpus Christi College, Oxford 34, 75, 190
Costin, William 48, 62
Counterfactuals 168–70
Counter-Reformation 2
Covenants 35, 87–8, 97, 116, 118, 126, 171, 182
Cranmer, bishop 2
Crossman, Richard 127–30, 133

D
Day, Peter 59, 61
de Walden, *see* Howard de Walden Estate

Delaune, William 15–16
Dibdin, Thomas Frognall 17–19
Dillenius, Johann 19
Discipline 5, 161–2
Dissolution of the Monasteries 4
Dogs 23–4, 56
Donations, *see* Gifts
Done, J. J. 37
Dr Radcliffe's School 106
Dowson, Philip 65–6

E
Eagle ironworks 95–6
Election
  to the St John's presidency 62–4, 150, 154, 165
  to the University Chancellorship 159–60
Eliot, George 25
Elizabeth I 2, 4
Endowment, *see* Finances of St John's
Engineering Department, *see* Thom Building
Esher, Lord, *see* Brett, Lionel
Eton College 36–7, 47, 57, 106, 173–4, 178–80
Eveleigh, John 19
Examinations 14–17
  collections 144, 163

215

reformed 7, 19
results of 139, 141, 149–50, 152–3, 159, 163–4

F
Fabians 124
Felixstowe Dock 107, 175
Fell, Charles Yates 38, 139
Fellowship of St John's College 29, 33, 40, 46, 48, 56, 60, 62–3, 65, 85, 94, 96, 98, 109, 123, 135–9, 141–2, 149, 151, 154, 161, 163, 165, 171, 173, 181
Fellowships 4, 20–1, 24–6, 146–7
Fereday, Dudley 25
Finance Committee 51–2, 59, 90, 94
Finance Office 168n2, 190
Finances of St John's 9–10, 18, 24, 26–9, 41–2, 44, 56–7, 64–6, 68, 71–2, 81–3, 85, 89–94, 97, 103–5, 107, 109–10, 189–91
Financial assets
  commercial property 89
  equities 51, 68, 71–2, 74–8, 81, 83, 85, 89–92, 103, 109
  fixed income 51, 71–3, 76–7, 81–2, 85, 90–2, 103, 109, 122

housing 34–5, 51–2, 56–7, 59–60, 83, 85, 88, 94, 99–100, 109, 123
land 18, 27–30, 33–4, 41, 44, 73, 83, 85, 100, 104, 122
oil 78
Financial theory 80–1, 91–3, 108, 137
  total return 81–2, 101
First World War 42–4, 80–1, 88, 112, 114, 124, 126, 134, 169
Foster, John 132
Founder, *see* White, Sir Thomas
Franks Report (1966) 144
Fraud 42
Front Quadrangle 193
Fyfield 101–2, 109

G
Gaitskell, Hugh 128
Garrard, Arthur 50, 55–6, 58, 64, 94, 99–102, 104–7, 178, 181
Gayton, Edmund 11–12
George, Henry 112, 123
Ghosts, *see* Haunting
Gibbon, Edward 11
Gibbons, Orlando 6
Gifts 3, 6, 8, 10, 18–19, 25, 28, 41, 151

Gilbert and Sullivan 37
Gilts, *see* Financial assets
Gladstone, William 22
Glasson, W. J. W. 42
Glyn, Alan 119
Gold standard, departure from 77, 80
Governing Body of St John's College 52, 55, 59–60, 95, 104, 107, 144, 189
Graduate students 62, 139, 144
Griffiths, James 129
Grosvenor family 106, 116, 133, 172, 177–8

H
Harcourt, Lord 49, 53, 56, 103, 136
Hart-Synnot, R. V. O. 42, 93–4, 99
Haunting 8, 69
Hawkins, Edward 23–4
Hayes, William 46–7, 189
Henshaw, Benjamin 3
Henshaw, Thomas 3
Hertford College 156n12, 158–9, 161, 165
Heygate, William Edward 21–2
Horses 97

Housing association 58, 65, 106, 178
Howard de Walden Estate 171–2
Hutton, William 41

I
Investment sub-committee 65, 78, 190

J
James, Herbert Armitage 41
James II 10
Jenkins Committee 126
Jesus College 156n12
Johnson, R. W. 188–9
Jowett, Benjamin 23–5
  caricatured 26
Juxon, William 9–10

K
Kay, John 65, 190
Keble College 46–7, 98, 155, 157, 190
Keble, John 22–3
Kendrew, John 151, 189
Keynes, John Maynard 75, 77, 79, 81, 92–3, 188
Kidd, Harry 64, 105
King's College 75, 79, 81, 92, 188–9
Knox, Vicesimus 16–17

L

Labour Party 51, 54, 57, 106, 115, 126–32, 134, 136–7, 184
Lady Margaret Chair in Divinity 15
Lamb & Flag 48, 150
Lambeth Palace 9, 193–4
Land reform 111–14, 116, 124–5, 127
Land value tax 112, 123
Latimer, bishop 2
Laud, William 10, 69, 167
  at St John's 5–9, 12, 193–6
Leasehold reform 53–4, 56–7, 85, 88–9, 95, 104, 106, 110, 114–15, 122–34, 137–8, 142, 171, 175–84
Leases
  beneficial 29–32
  99-year 1, 35, 37, 44, 48, 51–2, 56–7, 66, 68, 73, 85, 87–8, 95, 117–18, 120–2, 126–7, 135, 171, 180–1, 184
  on flats 182–4
Liberal Party 124–5
  land campaign 112
Lincoln College 20
Lloyd George, David 112, 124
Lobbying 58, 103, 106–7, 131, 133, 175–9
London School of Economics 64
London Stock Exchange 76
Lord of the manor, *see* Social responsibility of ownership
Luard, Evan 131, 133, 176
Lunatics, society of 17–18

M

Mabbott, John 61–2
Magdalen College 32, 36, 153, 188–9
Markowitz, Harry 80–1, 91
Mary I 2
Marylebone 171–4
Maufe, Edward 46
McCallum, R. B. 77, 77n15
Merchant Taylors'
  Company 2
  School 3, 21, 24, 38
Merton College 29
Ministry of Agriculture 73–4, 78, 107–8, 151, 179
Ministry of Housing and Local Government 106, 127, 129, 176–7
Mitchell, Leslie 147
Monmouth's rebellion 10
Montgomery, John 65

N

New College 127–8
New economy bubble 190
Newman, John Henry 23

Index

Noetics 23–4
Norrington Table 68, 68n181, 139, 141, 147, 149, 151–3, 157n14, 158–9, 164
North Oxford 41, 44, 48–57, 59, 87–9, 93–8, 102–5, 107, 109, 113, 116, 121, 135–7, 168, 170–1, 174, 181–2
  building of 34, 36
  inhabitants of annoying 98–100
Novels
  Brideshead Revisited 42–3
  Godfrey Davenant at College 21–2
  The New Republic 25–6
  Oxford: The Novel 45, 45n136
  Patchwork 43
  Vile Bodies 43

O
Omond, T. S. 42
Oriel College 19–20, 23, 31n92, 32, 156
Owen, Thankful 10
Oxford Preservation Trust 49, 137
Oxford Union 141

P
Park Town 36
Parliament 31, 59, 107, 119, 130, 133–4, 138, 175
  challenging Charles I 6–8
Patience 37
Pattison, Mark 20, 23, 25
Pension funds
  Imperial Tobacco 76
  St John's 79
Pigeons 3, 98, 182
Pigs
  offensive and forbidden 180
  prize-winning 56
Poetry
  benign influence of 167
  malign influence of 11
Poke, Thomas 12–13
Political risk 51, 55, 87, 95, 114, 135, 137, 171, 179–80
Port Meadow 34, 50, 95
Prideaux, Humphrey 12
Princeton University 77
Prynne, William 6

Q
Queen's College, Oxford 31

R
Rack rents 30–3, 51–2, 60, 85, 94
Rawlinson, Richard 28
Religious purpose of University 23, 25–6

Rent control 51, 59–60, 88, 99–100, 114–15, 125, 175
Richardson, George 51–2, 54–6, 72, 83, 89–93, 95, 104, 109, 135–6, 180–1, 190
Ridley, bishop 2
Ridley, Sidney 90–3
Right to Buy 134
Rossi, Hugh 134
Royal Society 24, 46, 141
Rugby School 41
Ryde, Edward 35

S
St Anthony's College 131, 144
St Bernard's College 3–4
St Catherine's College 156n12
St Edmund Hall 47
St Giles 1, 18
St John's College, Cambridge 106, 176, 188
St Philip and St James Church 97–8
St Thomas 1
Salisbury, Lord 124
Scholarships 5, 24, 147, 152, 160–1
Second World War 44, 48, 75–6, 94, 133, 139, 155, 157
Select Committee on Town Holdings 35–6, 121

Sheep, generosity of 27
Shell, Royal Dutch 78
Sidney Sussex College 180
Silsoe, Lord 177
Sinking fund 73–4, 107
Sir Thomas White Building 62, 65–6, 68, 152–3
Slade, Edwin 60–1, 63
Smith, Adam 11
Social responsibility of ownership 29, 52–6, 87–9, 96–103, 105, 109, 137, 173
Southern, Richard 62, 65–6, 68–9, 139, 142–4, 147–55, 164–6, 189
Southwark 36
Speed, John 12
Stanley, Arthur Penrhyn 20
Statue
 St Bernard 4
 John the Baptist 3
Statutes
 of King's College 75, 79
 of Oxford 8
 of St John's 83, 89
Student life 2–3
Summertown 36

T
Tanner, Neil 158–9, 161, 165

Teaching 46–7, 61, 63, 139, 142, 144, 147–8, 153–4
  lectures 4
  purpose of 22
  spending on 40, 68, 152, 164
Thatcher, Margaret 134
Thom Building 50, 170
Thomas, George 132–3
Thomas, Keith 47–8, 64, 142, 148–9, 154, 165–6, 189–90
Thompson, Harold 47, 63–4, 148
Thorold Rogers, J. E. 123
Tommy White Quad, *see* Sir Thomas White Building
Tonbridge School 17
Tortoise 8–9
  metaphysical status of 193–6
Town plan, *see* City council
Townmaker 50
Tractarians 22–3, 98
Trevor-Roper, Hugh 63, 143, 159
Trinity College, Cambridge 75, 105–7, 175–6, 188
Trinity College, Oxford 34
Troops 10
Trusts
  at St John's 27–8, 77–9, 83, 89–90
  restrictions on investments 73–4, 77–9, 87, 89, 94

U
University College 20, 34, 65, 101n55, 147–9, 152, 156, 161, 165

V
van Tromp, Cornelis 12
Visitor of St John's 13

W
Wadham College 156n12
Wall Street Crash 92
Walton Manor 18, 89n36
  redevelopment of 50, 52, 58, 102–4, 135–8, 171, 174
Walton Well 96
Wasperton 28
Waugh, Evelyn 42–4
Western Ground Rents 117, 132–3, 176
Westminster, Duke of, *see* Grosvenor family
Westminster School 47, 160
Whately, Richard 23
White, John 47
White paper on leasehold reform 56, 85, 106, 181
White, Sir Thomas 2, 5, 18, 109, 154

Whitgift, archbishop 5
Wilderness, howling 35
Willey, Fred 129, 177–8
Wilson, Harold 127, 130, 177
Winchester School 128
Wolfson College 144
Wolvercote 1, 18, 72

Women
  colleges 46, 157
  in Oxford 13–14, 40–1, 100–1, 163–4
Wood, Anthony 11–12
Woodhouse, Montague 133–4